From Animal House
to the Academy

From Animal House to the Academy

Jeffrey J. Langan

Library of Congress Control Number: 2008903914
ISBN: Hardcover   978-1-4363-3834-9
                 Softcover   978-1-4363-3833-2

This book was printed in the United States of America.

To order additional copies of this book, contact:
Xlibris Corporation
1-888-795-4274
www.Xlibris.com
Orders@Xlibris.com
46573

To Marie, Catherine, and Katie, my first philosophical mentors.

"The true nature of man, his true good, true virtue, and true religion, are things we can only know inseparably." Pascal, *Penseés* 442

"And you he made alive, when you were dead through the trespasses and sins in which you once walked, following the course of this world, following the prince of the power of the air, the spirit that is now at work in the sons of disobedience. Among these we all once lived in the passions of our flesh, following the desires of body and mind, and so we were by nature children of wrath, like the rest of mankind. But God, who is rich in mercy, out of the great love with which he loved us, even when we were dead through our trespasses, made us alive together with Christ." Ephesians 2:1-5

INTRODUCTION TO THE ACADEMY

" THE SOUL THAT is under a tyranny will least do what it wants, speaking of the soul as a whole. Always forcibly drawn by its passions, it will be full of confusion and regret." Plato, *Republic*

"Now, he who exercises reason and cultivates it seems to be both in the best state of mind and most dear to the gods. For if the gods have any care for human affairs, as they are thought to have, it would be reasonable that they would delight in that which most resembles them, that is reason, and they will reward those who love and honor this most, as caring for the things that are dear to them and acting both well and nobly." Aristotle, *Nicomachean Ethics* X

Background

This book is based on the observations that senior students have made to me over the years, on my interactions with undergraduates, University graduates acquaintances or visitors, and people concerned about improving the education of young people.

I have put together this book based on their experiences, both positive and negative—what they were glad they did, or what they feel they missed. I have also tried to gather together what has led to students truly benefiting from their University experience, to the point that people who look at those students said that they have truly matured during their time at the University. This book primarily addresses students who are entering or who are in college and who want to make the most of these years. In your time at the University, you have the capacity to choose whether you will use time well or poorly. I hope to offer some suggestions that will help you use it well.

Looking back—the Good and the Bad

I cannot list all the ways things are done well or poorly. I do know, however, that there are typical mistakes we make in college. Some people look back on their University years and say, "Yes, I got drunk every weekend." I would probably not say that was the best use of their time. On the other hand, someone sent me an e-mail to say, "I look back and realize the most important thing that I did in my four years is I learned how to pray."

This is a fairly common statement among those who matured during their University years—they learned to pray or to grow spiritually during their time in college; and they considered that to be the most important thing they learned. Many others have the opposite observation—they look back and say, "You know, I realize I wasted my time." When we draw out the conversation, it's often revealed that what they mean is that they feel they failed to mature as much as they could have during their University years.

The "failures" oftentimes see that their problem relates to learning how to pray and to their spiritual growth, . . . but that is not all. Typically, people regret not using their summers or their breaks during their University years to travel or to do service projects. Others fail to account for the hidden biases in their instruction. When they are seniors, or after they leave the University, they realize, "Whoa! The whole time I was there I was manipulated by this or that ideological agenda." Still others waste their education by immersing themselves in one form of activism or another, leaving studying to a distant second, third or fourth place among their priorities.

In this book, I will propose a model whereby you can make the best use of your time while at a University so that you can mature as a person. I hope that you will be able to mature as a person so that you are ready for leadership. In some ways, you will be a leader whether you realize it or not, and how you shape your soul will influence other people, the culture and the institutions of our society for many years to come.

Other facets of University life that I will discuss are the relationships of friendship, dating and marriage. But probably the most important thing I hope this book will do is set you on the path to growing in virtue—to developing friendships of virtue, and to acquiring unity of life. Philosophy is a way of life. The true philosophy should affect the way you think and the way you act, no matter where you are or what you do, because philosophy helps you to understand reality and your place in it. When you understand this, you can more easily develop integrity. Integrity means you will be the same person at home, in the classroom, in the dorm, in the dining hall, while socializing, on the sports field, and out with your friends.

Develop the courage to be the same person at all times. Do not let fear of the wrong things govern your life. The man of virtue does not suppress his fear; he fears the right things and takes delight in the right things. He has the courage to overcome what is sometimes a fear: to learn and to bring his words and deeds into conformity with the truth of things, when he sees that he has somehow deviated from the truth of things.

College: Vacation or Vocation?

The book is intended to encourage you to start thinking now—"What are the ways that I can best use my college years?" It will return to this theme from many angles.

Your college years can be a great time in life. Many people look back and say that it was the best time of their lives. Unfortunately, for many people college is a vacation from life. They only appear to have fun. They really do not take it as seriously as they could. There are all sorts of ways in which they could use the time better to prepare for whatever they are going to do in life. There are all sorts of ways they could have real fun in college. But they fail to see how.

It can help to think about college as a preparation for a vocation. A vocation is something that someone is called to do. It is a purpose that each of us has. When we are young, we do not know what this is. We might have a sense of what it is based on our inclinations, interest, and self-knowledge. Part of what we want to do in college is to more readily define our vocation and prepare for it, no matter what it happens to be. In part, this is why we take classes and study. We want to understand the human person better, the universe, and the role of the person in society. As you learn, at some point, you will ask yourself, "How do I fit into this picture?," or, in other terms, "what is my vocation? What am I asked to do in this world?" You will be asked this in your first job interview, when your potential employer will ask you "Why do you think you should work for this company?"

Culture and Leadership

Of course our education and our life is more than the first job we are going to get. Another important issue for us to consider now is culture and leadership. Today it seems the vision of leadership that is being proposed to us is to do whatever you need to do to get into your field, to become an astronaut or to get into Hollywood, even if it means doing vulgar, immoral, or unjust things. Even worse, some people adopt an attitude of indifference, thinking or saying that we do not even need to figure out whether what we are doing is good or evil.

There is a danger in this mentality; it can lead to blindness to the harm that you do to yourself and to others. It can also lead to blindness to the ways that others are harming or using you. It sometimes seems that we are being trained to be pawns or instruments that carry out the wishes of others who have neither the common good nor our good in mind. We think we need to have a good reputation with the leaders in order to have power and influence. But we think that we have to sacrifice our good in order to get these positions of power and influence. The graphic example is that of Catholic actors and actresses who feel pressured to do immoral things in order to get leading roles. But, there is a little of that compromise that goes on in every profession. Sometimes, a person simply wants security or a feeling of being wanted, and he sacrifices his own good in order to be accepted by others. This happens often at college, either at a party or in an individual relationship with friends or with professors.

Sometimes, we simply want to live comfortable lives. Therefore, we do not want to take risks, as the easy path is clearly before us. And so, we have a tendency to stay out of leadership positions. We do not want to risk it, especially in areas of cultural leadership. It might also be true that Catholics are excluded from such positions, but often, we do not even try. Or, when we were young, we were so distracted by other things we made ourselves incapable of being a leader. Rather than focusing on doing well in our studies and a few extracurricular activities, we overcommitted ourselves to so many activities that rather than thinking through how best to become a leader, we spent our time rushing around from one activity to the next, not knowing how or why we were doing what we were doing.

Let me provide an example. While planning this seminar, I contacted a friend who is in contact with more than 3,000 Christian men. I enquired about bringing in professional Christian men in various areas who can help some students, give talks, and help students think about, and prepare for, professional life. Among others, I asked for men in media, entertainment, journalism, service professions and public relations. The e-mail I got back was, "I don't know exactly what you are looking for . . . we don't know anybody in those professions. I know one guy who was involved in PR (a public relations company), and he is retired now. If you want doctors, engineers, and lawyers, and businessmen we have got lots of those types."

This explains a lot. As we look out at our culture, at the University, or at other fields such as Hollywood entertainment, politics or journalism—at the professions that truly shape the culture and institutions of a society over time—it seems that good people do not get into leadership roles in these professions.

It is not bad—in fact, it is important—that Catholics become businessmen, engineers, and follow other such productive occupations. But it is a little bit of a travesty that out of 2,000 to 3,000 Catholic men in a major city, no one is involved in the entertainment business, either on the business side or on the creative side. It is hard to find a journalist. We have to scrape the bottom of the barrel to find competent Catholic mathematicians and scientists who can carry out their teaching and research while living intellectual and moral unity with their Catholic faith. There are probably Catholic people working in the military. I would imagine if we looked at politics and business more closely, we would see many Catholics in these professions. However, they are not the leaders in their professions—they are carrying out someone else's orders. Again in athletics sometimes you will see a good Catholic sports coach, or a good coach who is dominant. But oftentimes on the business side it tends to be more oligarchic or amoral.

Caring for our souls

Someone might think that the reason that Catholics fail to control the culture is because we fail to have power and laws on our side. This is only part of the truth. Often we do not become leaders, and we do not take control of our culture because we have disordered souls. We fail to live virtue, so we fail to have the true strength of character that enables us to be real leaders; unbending and generous when it comes to doing what is good and avoiding evil. We also fail to see or account for the variables or the circumstances that make up our situation. And, we would rather live a comfortable life than do something risky. Hopefully, this situation will change. I know of some Christian men and women who are doing some very risky things right now.

This reality or problem is an opportunity for you. Victor Hugo once wrote that the book had replaced the cathedral as the source of meaning in the West. This led Frank Lloyd Wright to return architecture to its place of prominence. Mark Twain wanted to be a philosopher or a writer. He chose to be a writer as a way of transforming society by his ideals. You, Catholic student, you should look at the world and decide how you are going to change it. Only you, if you understand yourself and reality, will change it for the better.

What you need is not simply an orientation to college that tells you where the dining hall is, how to get to class, how to write your resume, and what groups to join. You need an orientation that presents before you the challenge of your times, how to develop your soul during your University years, and why it is urgent for you to think perhaps in a more magnanimous way than those around you.

Plato had this idea: Too many people think that to get ready for society we need to develop skills, such as how to balance a checkbook, or how to make presentations, and so forth. Napoleon Dynamite summed it up when he compared all of these skills to nunchuck skills. Young men should not be primarily or exclusively concerned with developing skills. These skills are important, but they are not the most important thing that a young man needs in his life. What he really needs to worry about, especially when he is between the ages of 14 and 22, is how to care for his soul and become a man of integrity. Frank Lloyd Wright decided when he was 14 that he was going to transform the world of architecture. If only he had, at that time, also chosen that he was going to transform his soul through the life of virtue, how much different modern architecture would be now.

We need to bring unity to our lives. So often we live compartmentalized lives. You are one personality at home, another in school, a third on the sports field, a fourth playing video games, a fifth with the girls, and a sixth at parties. You are not the same person everywhere and with everybody. You lack unity of life. Someone who has unity of life knows how to harmonize his behavior so that he is the same person no matter where he goes and what he does. He lives virtue everywhere, in the appropriate way, according to the circumstances.

To develop unity of life, you need to start cultivating virtue now. You need to learn how to make choices that make demands on yourself *now*, to create a kind of discipline within our souls right now. You need to do this now, so that when you are older you do not project your lack of discipline or vice onto the world in whatever jobs or positions you end up in. You also need to develop the capacity to see your job or profession in the light of the fullness of reality, rather than only a part of it. Finally, you need the strength, the vision, and the magnanimity to be able to act in such a way that you can change your profession.

Moreover, vice, any vice, blinds you to the harm you do to yourself. In as much as you possess vices, you are blind to the harm you do to your soul and to the harm you do to others. You are also more easily controlled by others. Someone else can control you by threatening to take away from you that false desire that you think you need. The opposite is true, and in as much as you acquire virtue, you are free. You are not controlled by anybody else. And you do good to, rather than harm, those around you.

Pitfalls of University Life

This book is negative, in the good sense of the word. It sets out to expose the mentalities that we want to avoid, as well as to explain how some of those mentalities have been reinforced in our educational institutions over the past few hundred years.

If we really want to be honest with ourselves we have to admit that the modern University environment, for all of its great advances, has aspects that are morally corrupt and corrupting. Corruption means that an individual or a society has adopted bad habits and practices and the leaders and citizens no longer recognize them as bad. There are many vicious, corrupt, or even depraved customs that are part of the modern University and we should become aware of this as soon as possible. Educators often have difficulty helping students root out these bad habits because the educators themselves have adopted philosophies that support rather than root out the bad habits. In addition, there is always an element of free choice involved. You are ultimately the one who has to choose whether you want to live virtue or not. You are free to choose whether you want to mature into a free person or remain an animal the rest of your life.

The risk we run is being indifferent or blind in the face of corrupt customs and then we could adopt them into our own lives, bringing about much damage to our souls and, in turn, inflicting much harm on others during our college years and in our professional, family and social lives later on. The danger, as Plato reminds us, is in following these corrupt ideas, only to learn much later on, in the sad school of experience, how much damage they do to us and the harm they enable us to inflict on others.

Become aware of the corrupting influences as soon as possible in your college career. Why? Because they exist all around us. The college environment is like a fish tank. Some friends of mine once bought a fish tank. The first week they owned it, they had a party. The attendees at the party started dissolving gummi bears into the fish tank. Then, they poured a little liquor into the tank. They wanted the fish to enjoy the fruits of the party. The gummi bear dissolved in the water and the next day we noticed that the fish were still alive, but they were sucking for air. A lot of times if we do not prepare ourselves properly we will be like those fish, just sucking for air the whole time.

At the same time, if we can describe the problem, we can start to take the steps to fix it. I remember growing up in Detroit, and how people used to joke about the Detroit River catching fire. There was so much pollution in the river that people could see small fires on the river. But at some point, the citizens of Detroit stopped laughing and decided to do something about it. They controlled the pollution and cleaned up the water. There is an analogy between the physical environment and the moral environment. The moral environment right now is like the Detroit River in the 1970s. We need to clean it up. If we fail to clean up our moral environment, our soul, then fires will start to flare up in our lives, some of them not so laughable. But, if we set out now to identify the sources of pollution, we can cut them off, and let nature purify the rivers of water that will flow through our soul and clean it.

We have to figure out not only how to survive, but also how to transform our culture and transform the University environment such that the water becomes clean again. Once they stopped the pollution flowing into the

Detroit River, nature took its course. Nature on its own could help restore her river to a better state.

Again, there is an analogy here. There are tried and true ways, natural ways we can become, and do become, leaders. These tried and true ways are the ways of acquiring virtue. Perhaps the best guides for growing in virtue, especially when the environment is polluted, are given to us by Plato and the Catholic Church. The Church has thousands of years of experience helping souls learn how to mature. So it makes a lot of sense, even if we are not Catholic, to look at the Church from the point of view of understanding how it helps us to grow in virtue.

We shall also see that one of the big reasons we have the polluted culture that we do is due to a sometimes explicit effort to remove from the University system and from the culture at large the vision of virtue as taught by the Catholic Church or any philosophy that seems compatible with the Catholic Church's approach to life. Thus, in part, the moral environment has been polluted because there are conscious and sometime subconscious efforts, but efforts nonetheless, to remove a particular philosophy from leadership status in society. If this is the case, then the only way you will acquire it is if you take the time to learn it and acquire it. The only way it will influence leaders again is if the leaders themselves learn it and live it.

CHAPTER ONE

" C ONSIDER WELL THE seed that gave you birth:/ you were not made to live your lives as brutes,/ but to be followers of virtue and wisdom." Dante, *Inferno* XXVI

The Institutions that Build a Society

Plato observed that in any society there are certain institutions which, over time, are shaped by the souls of the leaders of these institutions. If you want to tell the direction that society is going, all you need to do is look at the character of the souls of the leaders of the various institutions. These institutions really have an effect on the character of the people, on the laws and on the customs of a society over time.

If we performed a sociological analysis, and made Plato contemporary, what would he say are the most formative institutions of a country's political structure, of a country's make-up, the character of the people? Probably one of the most formative would be what he calls poetry. We would translate poetry into music, literature, film, television, theatre, journalism—entertainment in general. The second area that shapes institutions, customs, and law over time is the military. The third would be business leaders, and the fourth area would be political leaders. The last area could be termed "others"—athletics, athletic leaders, and similar professions.

Plato then talks about the standards by which we can judge a society.

If you look at human experience you realize that many people argue that everything is relative. However, before you concede the argument of the relativist, it would be good to first think with him and say, "I am ready to admit that everything is relative but before we say everything is relative, what are the actual standards by which people judge behavior?"

We should not be relativists out of ignorance. Let us not be relativists just because we are stupid. Let us be relativists because we have thought about this experiential question. What is a standard, and what are the actual standards, based on everyday experience, by which people can judge their behavior? Relativism means there are either no standards or so many standards that we cannot choose between them.

This is one of the purposes of Plato's "The Republic": To think through the actual standards by which people judge their actions or judge their souls to be just. Only after we think through the possibilities, can we then make some sort of intelligent claim about relativism.

Five standards to judge behavior

In Book 8 of "The Republic" (which my students say is the best—it is the easiest to understand and makes the most sense), Socrates identifies five basic standards by which humans judge behavior. He admits that there might be more. In my opinion, these five are pretty comprehensive. If you look at every profession and if you look at society as a whole over time, you can identify where that profession is on this scale. If you add all the professions together, you can get a sense of what society as a whole is like right now.

The standards are:

(1) Virtue: When a person, family or a profession is virtuous, or when a society as a whole is virtuous, what does that mean? It means that there are habits or dispositions to do what is good in that person or group of people. It also means that the society (or profession or person) does whatever it does, based on whether or not it is just or unjust, based on whether or not it is evil or good.

(2) Timocracy: this is the society in which men and women judge their behavior based on honor or reputation or glory. Beating people in competition; winning the Super Bowl; being known as that guy who has always been known as a good guy—these are instances of timocratic behavior. The generation of the Depression and World War II in the United States—the "Great Generation," was, on the whole, a timocratic generation.

(3) Oligarchy: In an oligarchic soul, family, profession or society, wealth and comfort become the standard by which we judge whether an action is good or bad. If it makes money and leads to comfort it must be good. If we fail to make money and fail to become comfortable it must be bad.

The Greek term for Oligarchy is actually very much related to Timocracy. The implication of the word is that the person uses money to buy honor or to buy reputation.

(4) Democracy: Democracy is when pleasure becomes the standard by which we judge whether something is good or bad. Socrates says that democracies will be multicolored or multicultural. They did not have the word culture at the time, but multicultural would be the most likely term these days. In a democracy the citizens give equal rights to all the passions. Every passion has the same rights as every other passion.

(5) Tyranny: Tyranny is when power becomes the standard of what is good and what is evil.

The United States and the Five Standards

As soon as a person, family or profession departs from the standard of virtue, usually the first standard he will appeal to is honor or reputation. The person or institution will become timocratic. Virtue is already present in timocratic souls but it is less than true virtue. Timocratic souls are more worried about their reputation and the honor that they receive than about truly doing good or evil.

You can see this happening in the history of our country. Sometime during the nineteenth century we became an oligarchy. What was good and bad was determined by seeking wealth. By the twenties, democracy emerged in our society. The Protestants started losing their faith. The elites—the people who run politics, culture, journalism, Hollywood—started to lose their faith. They began to be very much ruled by pleasure as a standard of behavior.

The Depression and the Second World War returned people to a kind of basic timocracy, for Catholics at least—not to virtue but to timocracy. Many people of those generations did many noble and honorable things, often without realizing what they were doing. Timocracy is not bad—it is sometimes the closest you can get to virtue.

In a timocracy, over time, the oligarchic tendency starts to take over. In our society, this happened by the late fifties or sixties. Socrates speaks of the mother who loves her husband but starts to complain to her children that Father does not make enough money and does not buy her enough things; or that Father cannot buy her all the things that she wants.

Thus the child almost imperceptibly lets the desire to make money overtake his soul. The child of the man who is honorable and noble sets out to make money. By doing so, he feels he is going to buy the honor or nobility that his Father always lived with but was never recognized for; that he is going to buy the reputation his Father never had.

When this child gives in to making money, his children look at their father and say, "Look, you have given in, in an unrestrained way, to following the desire for making money. What is the difference between you following money making and me following taking drugs or experiencing whatever pleasure I want to experience—sexual pleasure, gratification, and all these other things?"

Therefore, there will come a time when the oligarchic society will shift to become more of a democratic society. In 1968, America shifted from an oligarchy to more of a democracy.

Socrates says that in a democratic culture the children will become lotus eaters (a lotus was an opium or narcotic of the ancient world). The children of the sixties were democrats as young men. According to Socrates, a lot of people who are democrats when young become oligarchs when they turn forty, fifty and sixty. Then they will fight against their own kids who are democrats. Some parents may remain democrats throughout their lives. In turn, their children will become oligarchs—money makers. Thus, there will be tension back and forth between oligarchs and democrats for several generations.

Eventually, democracy will win out. When that happens, the stage is being set for tyranny in a society. The rule of a man who is a demagogue—someone who can tell the many exactly what they want to hear and then when he gains power he rules simply on the basis of power—becomes imminent.

The Five Standards applied to Western Society

European history

The nobility of England consists of families that Henry VIII had made into nobility by stealing land from the Church and giving it to these people. Almost every significant modern English name belongs to one of these families. The Cecils and the Stanleys were all families who were made nobles during the process of the Reformation.

When you study European history you will see that much of the way the process of Reformation succeeded was that the King or Kings in virtue-oriented or timocratic society tried to make a new class of oligarchs, so that they warred against the timocrats or the virtue-oriented people. In almost every reformation society there is a movement towards oligarchy. Most modern political battles are fought between oligarchs and democrats. The oligarchs are the conservatives and the democrats are the liberals.

Sports

Most athletes are entering the stages of democracy, if they are not already there yet. However, there will always be an element of timocracy in athletics.

In the hockey hall of fame at Toronto there is a little exhibit about the history of hockey. In the late nineteenth century, Lord Stanley (who hails from one of the aforementioned noble families of England) instituted the Stanley Cup in the 1880s. His idea was that the different cities which played hockey would compete once a year just for the cup.

Throughout the 1880s and 1890s, all these different cities—some in America, most in Canada—would compete for the Stanley Cup. In the early twentieth century an oligarch arose in the hockey world and he started to try and buy all these franchises and players. As he started making money, he went west. By the 1920s, there were hockey franchises in Vancouver, Poland and Seattle. These western franchises won a number of Stanley Cups.

By then hockey began to become very competitive. In the 1920s, the oligarchs basically took over hockey and started competing for players. There was no loyalty anymore—players would go from one team to the next and betray their cities. There was a great escalation in players' salaries. There was also a great escalation in the number of teams.

When the Depression hit, all that fell apart and the National Hockey League was reduced to eight teams. These teams returned to a more timocratic way of playing hockey. It remained that way until the late 1960s when they began adding on more teams again. In the 1970s, the competition between the oligarchs began again. They also began to explore the game as a kind of entertainment. Now hockey is right on the verge of becoming democratic—trying to appeal to everything and everyone, exuding sex appeal and becoming entertainment.

If you listen to ESPN radio you realize that they are blatant about making sports into a kind of entertainment. They always advertise in a subtle way or use sex to sell sports. If you follow almost any sport you will see that almost every sport goes the same way—from timocracy to oligarchy to democracy.

Science

Almost every profession is going the same way as sports. A scientist who spoke at Notre Dame last year complained about how in the early and middle twentieth century there were a lot of scientists who were simply scientists for the sake of winning glory for their country. They just wanted to be the first to discover penicillin, or the first to do this or that—not because they wanted to make money, but simply because they wanted to win glory for their country.

He said that nowadays one of the problems with a lot of things in science is that scientists are just doing things for money from the drug companies. Often, making money for the drug companies is not the best thing for the pursuit of science. Therefore, science is becoming democratic.

Entertainment and Military

I would argue that right now the entertainment industry is clearly democratic. I think it is a tragedy that it is hard to find Catholics in journalism, in entertainment, on any side—business or creative, in theater, film, television or the movie industry. I once read an article about two corrupt screenplay writers who were always working on screenplays and said they never watch TV or even go to movies. They supposedly spent all of their time writing the scripts that everybody else is going to look at.

There is always going to be an element of timocracy in the military. But when there are no wars going on, the military tends to become oligarchic or democratic.

Politics and Business

Over time, politics is becoming more democratic. Most business companies are oligarchic. However, a lot of leaders in businesses are democratic in their moral outlook. Bill Gates and Ted Turner and Warren Buffet have no moral standards at all. These are the business leaders of today.

With this scenario in mind, we will discuss next what constitutes a true leader in today's environment, and how you can be a leader in your chosen profession.

CHAPTER TWO

" THE TRUTH IS so obscured in our day, and falsehood so firmly established, that unless one loves the Truth, one cannot even know it." Pascal, *Penseés* 864

"War within man between reason and the passions.
If he only had reason without passions . . .
If he only had passions without reason . . .
But having both, he cannot be without war, not being able to have peace with one except by having war with the other." Pascal, *Penseés* 412

Preparing for Leadership Roles

This chapter begins to discuss who a leader is, and how you can lay the groundwork during your college years to become a leader in life.

Consumerist Culture

According to Plato, the happiest person is the person who acquires virtue. Virtue enables the person to experience friendship with the Divine Being. It prepares the person to see reality clearly. It also prepares the person to be capable of serving society and others in a way that builds up the common good, creating the possibility for concord and peace. The standard of virtue is the highest standard by which we can hold ourselves and judge human behavior. Of course, there are deviations from that standard. The timocratic soul judges his or her behavior by reputation, not virtue. This is common with sports programs and democratic politicians, who are often concerned about what the public at large thinks of their wins and losses on the sports field and in the political arena. Next up, we have the oligarchic soul, that judges behavior based on money or efficiency. Then, we have the democratic soul, which judges human action based on the pleasure it gives or whether all of the passions, not just the money-making one, have an equal opportunity to be recognized and fulfilled by the person and by persons in society. Democratic societies are multi-colored in that they provide for the freedom for each to follow his passions to the highest degree possible. Finally, there is the tyrannical soul. The tyrannical soul is the soul in which the predominant passion is the thirst for power.

Our culture trains us to become consumers, that is, it trains us to be oligarchs or democrats, and, as we shall see, the tyrannical soul can also find a home in our society, even if his or her desires for power are not as openly violent as they were during the time of the Athenian Empire. So, in our society the emphasis is: "What kind of music do you listen to? What kind of songs do you listen to? Who do you cheer for? Do you like this? Do you like that?"

In our culture we are trained to evaluate ourselves based on whether or not we are consuming properly. We often fail to think, "What does it take for me to become someone who is not a consumer; to become someone who is not doing the bidding of somebody else?" What does it take for me to understand what profession I want to go into? Can I see it from the vantage point of a leader in that profession, understanding the causality of that profession? Do I know what makes this profession tick?

The true people who rule the world are people who are 50 years old and over. Ideally, we should be preparing ourselves so that when we are 50 years old we are one of the leaders in our chosen field.

Nerds win the ball game

A professor on my dissertation committee likes to begin one of his first lectures by giving a short biography of each of the members of the Supreme Court. He brings out what these people did in college—what nerds they were and how nerdy they had been their whole lives. He describes Justice Souter as drinking a glass of milk every night and living with his mother. Souter went to Northwestern Law School. He studied, he never went out on the weekends, and so he was a nerd. He always ends this lecture with the point: "Nerds win the ball game!"

To some degree my professor friend is right. It is not the people who are rushing around all the time in college that are going to become leaders. It is the nerds, the people who become really enthusiastic about what they study and who commit themselves to becoming the experts in their field. *Nerds win the ball game!* This tongue in cheek example is only meant to show that you can spend time in college not simply being a nerd, but being concerned with building virtue in your soul. This may or may not lead you to the Supreme Court. But, if you can grow in virtue and if you end up on the Supreme Court the order in your soul will reflect itself into the Court Room and into law and society in profound ways for the good of society. The same is true of all the professions.

Catholics in Academia—sobering statistics

Why are only 40% of the professors Catholic at a typical Catholic university? At the top universities in the country why do Catholics make up 6% of the faculty? Part of it could be because, admittedly, there is an anti-Catholic bias in academics. But the other reason is that Catholic universities are notoriously bad at sending their students on to graduate school in academics. I know of one university that has a program of 600 Political Science majors. And in a typical year, three or four of this 600 will go on to graduate school in Political Science.

In comparison, if the average school like Arizona State would have 100 political science majors, they would send maybe between four and six to graduate school. So if they were to have 600 it would be multiply that by six and they would have 20 or 30. This school has a reputation for being a party school. Yet, more students from this party school go on to higher studies than from a typical Catholic university.

This is not to say that it is impossible for Catholics to cultivate students who can do graduate research. It can and is done at some places. The best Catholic school for sending students on to academic degrees such as PhDs is Thomas Aquinas College. Their percentage of students who advance to get PhDs is higher than the University of Chicago's. Thomas Aquinas has about 60 students per class and 12% of this number (around seven) goes on to get PhDs—more than that start out in graduate school. So one school with a raw number of 60 students beats out the political science department at a large Catholic University.

Risk taking and leadership

This trend toward consumerism rather than leadership in our chosen professions is endemic to almost every discipline. It's a sign of the culture. It is part of why we often spurn the more intellectual professions for professions in which we can earn more money. Our culture is preparing people to want to live comfortable lives. To dream of becoming a leader in your profession, even if it is technical like engineering, or to dream of being a leader in society through public relations, media, or entertainment requires risk. If your goal in life is to live a comfortable life you are not going to take risks. You are going to take the easy path.

A counterpoint, though, is that there are a lot of people with a Nietzschean mindset subverting the culture. In a democratic and consumer culture like our own, it has not been difficult for some to appear as democrats but who really harbor tyrannical intentions of subverting traditional customs and morality that protect the family and cultivate good citizens. Often, under the guise of making culture more "multi-colored" these individuals can actually use subtle techniques of propaganda and image manipulation to encourage us all to think of ourselves as consumers, driven by the need to slake our passions in the next stream that we see." The Nietzscheans seek to make culture more "multicolored," as Socrates would say. They commit themselves to professions, such as education, media, journalism, advertising, fashion, and entertainment. They are using their time in better ways to plan and carry out their mission in life. If we are more interested in avoiding risks and in living a comfortable life, the Nietzscheans will always win. It will be the disorder in their souls that makes its way like a wave through society.

Professions that influence the soul

You can see that there is an argument or point that I am building up to. While I have great respect for all professions, it is not hard to see that there are some professions in which it is perhaps more apparent how the order or disorder in the souls of the leaders of those professions can have a greater impact on the formation of law, education, and culture. And so, I encourage you to think about going into professions that have a greater influence on the soul. In some cases, these professions are less attractive from the financial standpoint. They do not promise the hopes of a comfortable life and a six or seven figure salary—everybody always makes the excuse of avoiding or leaving these professions because they say they cannot afford it. These professions are those such as journalism, the media and all of its facets, getting a PhD and being a professor of any sort, politics of any sort, and teaching. In all of these professions, in the course of your life, you will have the chance to deal with and shape many souls—these are the leadership professions, in some sense.

Catholics in this country have been notoriously bad at going into these professions without being sycophants. A sycophant is someone who panders to those in power in order to win favor with them. When I think of the first Christians, especially the martyrs, I often think that they were not sycophants. They had definite ideals about changing the ancient culture and rather than pander to it they confronted it precisely in the ways that ancient culture failed to be fully human. Sometimes it cost them their jobs and even their lives, but they did not back down in the face of obstacles and difficulties.

In the *Confessions,* Augustine tells the story of Victorinus. He was a professor at an Academy during the reign of Julian the Apostate. He was thinking of converting to Catholicism, but then, Julian issued a decree that Catholics had to leave their posts at the Academy. The reason given was that Catholics showed themselves to be intolerant and unable to live a healthy neutrality towards the other religions of the Empire. Augustine describes how Victorinus wavered but eventually became Catholic, even at the cost of his job.

Someone might say that Victorinus lost out on his opportunity to influence Roman Culture, though I would say that in the long run, the Romans, by doing what they did to Victorinus and others like him, only paved the way for their own demise. They showed their lack of nobility and justice, leading to the eventual crumbling of Roman institutions because people lost confidence in those institutions. The actions of Victorinus will forever be remembered in the *Confessions*, and a great reminder to us of the potential sacrifices we should be willing to make in order to remain committed to seeking the truth and living a life of virtue.

Perhaps there are the most obstacles placed in the way of someone who wants to enter the leadership professions and live like the first Christians. Those who enter these professions have to expect the same kind of setbacks as the first Christians. There were times during the Roman Empire, for example, that converting to Christianity meant losing an academic position.

I encourage you to think about these professions. The best approach here is to say, *"If we are going to change our civilization and return it to a Christian order, which is the most human and noblest order, it requires that the people who go into these professions have well-ordered souls."*

As in all professions, the people in these professions project their souls into their work. So, we need people to go into these jobs, who instead of projecting their disorder into their work, will instead project order. Also, we should remember that there were times during the first ages of Christianity when Christians were known to spread their faith through their professions, by their good example and the right words said at the right moments. We should not be afraid of setting this kind of example when we go into these professions.

LEADERSHIP MODELS

When you think about your life, therefore, you should think about next year, the next five years, the next 20 years, and the next 50 years. In fact, many students have found it to be an enlightening exercise to take 30 minutes or an hour or two sometime during each year of their college career to chart a potential course for their lives, imagining at what age they would get married and start a family, start a career, have grandchildren, and what they would hope to accomplish with their lives. It is a great way of thinking about what the real end or the purpose of your life is, what you want to be known as, and what you want to be remembered for. Often, after such reflection, it becomes easier to think about what are and are not beneficial ways of organizing your life in college. What you will do as you schedule each day in the present depends on the orientation that you can give yourself as far as becoming a leader in the future.

What models will you pursue to develop into a leader? It might be interesting to look up some of the following things:

o   What are the requirements for the Rhodes Scholarship. What are they looking for? How do you get a Rhodes Scholarship? What are the requirements for the forms?

o   What would take to become a Diplomat? One of the big features of becoming a Diplomat is that you would have to take the Foreign Service Exam. So how would one prepare for the Foreign Service Exam?

o   What would it take to go to MIT for graduate school? What are they looking for? What would it take to go to a top graduate school in the humanities, in order to become a professor of history, literature, philosophy, or in one of the social sciences?

o   What would it take to go to NYU or USC film school? Related to that—what would it take to go into the film industry, because maybe the best way is not to go to film school! Maybe, as a friend of mine told me, only losers go to film school! The real great directors perhaps tell people they do something else. What would it take to get involved in the film industry?

o   What is a Fulbright Scholarship? Are there any Fulbright opportunities for undergraduates? What are the opportunities that your University has for funding undergraduate student research?

o   How would you start an NGO—a Non Governmental Organization? How would you become a United Nations translator? What would it take to qualify?

o   How do the professions deal with the media? What does it take to write a press release? What are some of the things to keep in mind when writing a press release? How could a group of students run a public relations campaign? How could a group of students effectively deal with the media? Related to this, look up the criteria for getting into Columbia Journalism School.

Obviously if any of you could do these things it would be impressive, but you are not a failure if you do not do it. Hopefully, what we will gather are some of the criteria, or some of the models of what it means to be a man—something we can think of becoming some day.

These are some of the highest things we can aspire to that tend to turn out individuals who work in professional areas that have an impact on souls. Columbia Journalism School, the Fulbright Scholarship, Rhodes Scholarship, going to USC or NYU film school or working at the United Nations. To really do these things, you would have to become a leader, you would have to use your time well as an undergraduate, and you would have to think about your undergraduate career as more than just getting ready for your first job. You would have to think about your time as an undergraduate as more of a preparation for some great adventure. You have to be willing to make sacrifices now to become the kind of person who could compete for these things. At the same time, every profession needs a leader, someone who knows the principles of that profession, and who works in a way that draws others to follow him. You need to become that leader, and you can, if you start to take virtue seriously now.

Looking at the path to leadership now will give you an idea of what kind of a person you want to make of yourself in the next four or five years. Socrates, Plato, and Aristotle all recognized that a young person should strive to measure his actions against the Divine Being. This would lead the person to see that the highest thing in him is the part of him that is spiritual like the Divine Being, and that part of the person is the soul. The soul is the best, highest, and noblest part of the person. And so, the real leader, before all else, will cultivate his soul, to prepare his soul to see and befriend he Divine Being. In addition, the soul, in a real way, shapes society for better or worse, depending on the order that exists in it. We will see more in future chapters how this is so and why cultivating the soul is the most important task of a student at a university.

CHAPTER THREE

" THOSE WHO HAVE no experience of prudence and virtue, but are always living with parties and the like are, it seems, brought down by them and throughout life wander this way; but, since they don't go beyond this, they don't look upward toward what is truly above, nor are they ever brought to it; and they aren't filled with what really is . . . rather, after the fashion of cattle, always looking down with their heads bent to earth and table, they feed, fattening themselves, and copulating; and, for the sake of getting more of these things, they kick and butt with horns and hoofs of iron, killing each other because they are insatiable; for they are not filling the part of themselves that *is*, or can contain anything, with the things that *are*." Plato, *Republic*, Book IX

Let the time that is past suffice for doing what the Gentiles like to do, living in licentiousness, passions, drunkenness, revels, carousing, and lawless idolatry. They are surprised that you do not now join them in the same wild profligacy, and they abuse you; but they will give account to him who is ready to judge the living and the dead. I Peter 4:3-5

College: Vacation or vocation?

Orienting yourself to a life of leadership and virtue leads you to use time properly. On the other hand, a classic way in which people ineffectively use the time that they have is by just going from one thing to the next. They never take time to stop and think, "What do I need to do in the next six months or even in the next week; what do I need to do in the next eight weeks, in the next year, the next four years?"

We do not have to ask these questions every day but the best people in any profession, the ones that end up being leaders, are the ones that take an hour or two a week to rethink: "What is required of me right now? What do I need to do in the upcoming week?" They end up oftentimes with great peace and great serenity. They are able to address big challenges, and to take care of all the concerns they have in their lives.

The top CEOs of the most successful companies do not work 60 hours a week. They work 40 hours a week. They usually have two or three loves in their life. I was just reading about a CEO who said "I love my company, I love Harvard, and I love my wife." Those are the three loves in his life. Maybe that order is not the best order, but the point is that this guy was able to make time for all these things, and never seemed to work more than forty hours a week. He was the CEO of Philip Morris, which, in the last 25 years, has been one of the most successful companies in the world according to the book *Good to Great*.

The people who are leaders in almost every company are the people who can step back and plan out. They can plan out goals, they can plan out things to do each week, and how to allocate time each week to what are the things they need to do. They can plan out what they need to do next summer. Then they can look for the best things that help them make that plan. In short, they live at least one part of the virtue of prudence, which enables them to see the goal that they have in mind and to discern the best means to use to achieve that goal.

Here is a time line. I spoke about it in an earlier chapter. Take 10 minutes to plan things out a little bit.

2010	2015	2030	2040	2050-2060	2060-2070
	Marriage	40th Birthday 2-10 Children	Grandparent	Retirement	Dies Natalis

What is my, and what do I need to do to achieve my:

1 year Plan?

2 year Plan?

5 year Plan?

20 year Plan?

50 year Plan?

This is part of the life of leadership, the life of virtue. This is the kind of thing we are interested in.

Avoid Animal House

Nineteen sixty-eight was a decisive year in the history of the United States and Europe. To understand what led to that year and to understand its effects is something that would bring you much profit in your University years. That is when a good portion of the culture at the Universities became corrupt. What is corruption? Corruption is when you do what is evil but you no longer recognize it as evil. So in 1968, people began to do evil and they no longer recognized it as such or they began to rejoice in it, falsely thinking that evil would lead to happiness.

Another decisive year was the year of the movie *Animal House*, 1978. When I speak to professors who were around then and whom I respect, they say there was a noticeable difference in student behavior before and after *Animal House*. *Animal House* is a corrupt movie which a lot of students watched, and perhaps they still do. It became the ideal of what University life is supposed to be like—lots of drunken orgies, engaging in crazy acts of bestiality, parties all the time, complete craziness.

So the culture is set, and the customs at the Universities now are actually set, to encourage you towards vice, laziness, and lack of seriousness. Even some of the efforts made in Student Life to make things serious are really misguided. I do not think they are really getting at the heart of the problem. Oftentimes they just exacerbate the problem because they exacerbate the vicious tendencies that become part of the custom in a democratic culture. The mentality often is, "The *Animal House* culture or something worse has set in, we have to accept it and help the students enjoy that culture without criticizing it. The last thing we could ever do is directly oppose that culture or call it what it is and limit or end its corrupting influence."

Furthermore, University officials often adopt a relativistic standard towards student groups and student activities. It sometimes seems that the only groups and activities that are given money and support from the faculty and administration are those that further advance the *Animal House* agenda.

At this point, big things are probably not going to change in this area. Furthermore, there are many good things done by student life and activities, and there is no reason to go into a detailed analysis of what these groups do. The point to hone in on is your personal responsibility, the choice that you have to make whether you want to begin to live a life of virtue, a life of vice, or perhaps the worst of the three options, a double life.

Burn your boats

I want you to draw a line in the sand. Burn your boats. This refers to the famous story of Hernán Cortéz. Cortéz was the conquistador who came over from Spain and saw the barbarism that was going on at Mexico City. The Aztecs were sacrificing humans to appease their gods. Before doing so, however, the priests ripped the hearts out of their victims and chewed on them. Cortéz figured that something needed to change here. He might have had mixed motives, but that is not the point of this story. The point is, he saw a real injustice and committed himself and his men to ending it.

At one point his men were talking about going back to Spain. Cortéz sent back whoever wanted to go back. He said, "There is one boat going back, and whoever wants to go, get on the boat. We are going to burn the rest of the boats." He drew a line in the sand and basically said, "If you want to come with me, cross this line, come with me and we will take over Mexico City and win glory. We will put an end to the barbarism there. But if you want to go back you can all get back to the boats that are leaving, but we are burning the remaining boats . . . there is no turning back."

We are going to burn the boats . . . At some moment in your freshman year you will make a choice. It is the decisive choice of how you want to live your four years at the University. Do you want to live the four years as a party animal, or (a second choice which is I think is also equally poor) say, "I am not going to be a party animal but I am really going to be in both camps . . . I am going to be kind of a good guy. I will go to some parties and have a good time, relax and have fun and then I will pull all-nighters a lot because I am having fun. But I am not really going to take seriously growing in virtue, becoming a man, maturing."

The third option is, during your freshman year, to make a decisive choice and resolve, "I am a good person. I am going to become a good person while I am here. Sure, I am going to have fun while I am here, but this is also in some sense serious. To be serious, to grow in virtue, to learn how to be a man and to learn how to become someone who can serve others—someday my wife and my family—I have to start preparing for it now."

I will be honest with you. I have not seen many people honestly choose and follow through on the third option in my 12 years here, or in my 16 years of university life. I have seen some people do it, and they were and are very happy. So many people do not follow this option because there are so many distractions. It is hard to carve out time each day to think about things with a little serenity. You might think in any given week that you are missing out on that awesome party, that dance, that festival, playing pool, hitting the bars, playing video games together with the guys, extra-curricular activities, trips and so forth. There are thousands of good and not so good activities that can lead you away from or distract you from learning how to pray or growing in virtue.

Some of these things are not bad in themselves. But you can get so caught up in rushing from one thing to the next that in the end you never stop to think about what is important. You never make a commitment to grow. You become afraid of commitments because you want to experience all the pleasures that the multicolored life of the University has to offer you (remember the section on democracy?).

Start the journey to become a man

If in this day and age, in the wake of 1968, and after *Animal House*, you are going to take seriously the journey of becoming a man, you really have to do it on your own. The culture or customs are set to form you in vices rather than virtues. It takes almost heroic fortitude to go against vicious customs and culture. When I say on your own, I mean that you have to personally make the choice to live the life of virtue, and you have to seek the help so that you can do it. Many of the institutional sources simply have rejected the path of virtue or they do not know what it would mean to help a student down that path who chose that path.

There are some people who can support you, but very few intellectuals today know or care about what virtue is. There are very few people in the University you can go to. If you knocked at the door of even a rector at a dorm or someone in student life in a University, there would be a slim chance they could have an intelligent conversation or explain to you what virtue is. Even if they could define the term, they could not start explaining to you how to live virtue. Even if they could explain it to you, they may or may not be able to help you learn how to acquire and live the virtues.

This is because the customs, habits and traditions that have been part of education to help young men develop virtues have been eliminated from our theories of education and from the practice of education. It's also because of the *Animal House* culture, which is the standard of student life in many places. In fact, if you were to go to many of these administrators and indicate to them that you are interested in growing in virtue, they would think that you are strange, a reactionary, and that perhaps you need the help of a psychologist to overcome something they would term a disorder. Many are not just indifferent to the idea of virtue, they are hostile to it. So, all of this means that if you want to mature as a person you are going to have to seek your own resources for doing it. There are people who can help you, and you do need their help, but you will have to look for them. They are not simply set up in desks where you can go introduce yourselves to the coaches of virtue.

Set goals for your breaks

So, what can you do to learn about virtue and begin to live it? This book is here to help you identify your goals and then also to think about resources and what you need to do to obtain virtuous goals. One thing to think about is how you use your time outside the classroom on a daily, weekly, and yearly basis. Looking at the big picture, you can think about how to use your breaks. These can become great learning experiences. I am currently dealing with a number of sophomores who are already applying for summer internships and attending interviews. A lot of students are already signed up for service projects over fall break. Other students are already planning out: "Next year I might go study abroad," and things like that.

What's the best way to use your breaks? I have found over the years that the first summer of college is a very good summer to do a service project. The summer between sophomore and junior years is a very good summer to start doing internships.

Think about what you can do now to prepare for a life of virtue and leadership that you will not be able to do when you leave college. I have found over the years that something like summer service projects are very good for a student to do one summer or two summers during college. It is the kind of thing you will not have an opportunity to do after you leave college. It is also very good in college to plan out cultural and intellectual trips to foreign countries. Again it is something you will probably not have once you start to work, or once you get married. You will not have the opportunity to travel in the same way that you can travel when you are in college with a little bit of intellectual and cultural vision. When you are married and you travel you are usually always worried about your kids—it is just not the same thing.

Pitfalls for students

What are some of the pitfalls that students can fall into as they plan out their weeks, years and lives? They are the same pitfalls that are the obstacles to growing in virtue. The ultimate pitfall is to turn your soul over to a standard other than virtue for judging your goals, desires, and individual actions. In other words, to answer the question posed by relativism, there is a standard for judging our behavior. We should judge our actions according to the standard of whether they help us grow in virtue.

If we let our desires for money, success, power, reputation, or pleasure lead us to replace virtue as a standard for judging our actions, we are on the slippery slope that leads to destruction. We will not truly learn and our intellect will be blind to the truth of things. Our will will become weak. It will not only follow the desire we give in to at the moment, it will now more easily open itself to other desires. It will be weak in resisting other desires that it does not want to follow.

Worrying too much about money

Sometimes when we think about the disorders that can enter into the soul, we tend to focus on lust. For some young men, this is an obvious problem.

What we fail to realize, however, is that there are other desires that can lead to disorder in our lives. The desires can be both material and spiritual. For example, someone could be attached in a disordered way to his reputation, to what people think of him. He could be attached to reputation in such a way that he makes all of his choices based on what others think, not on what is true and good. Or, sometimes he will sacrifice what is true and good because he subordinates it to what others think. Then, there is the error of the young man who says he does not care about reputation, so he never accepts any criticism or guidance from anybody else. He does evil things without ever thinking through the effects of his actions, as if there were none.

Another desire is the love of money. This, actually, is a huge problem. Too many people think about profession, major, and life, subordinating other concerns to this desire. There are a lot of students who do not do what they could do to mature because they worry too much about money, and, in doing so, neglect developing their personalities.

We should avoid excessive concern about money. At the same time, we should not be fearful of a little debt. Usually a freshman in college feels daunted by the prospect of going into debt to pay for his education. The important thing here is to remember that you will have a job in three years. Here is a simple calculation that you can do on your own. Figure out how much an entry level salary is for a profession you are interested in right now. Then, figure out how much in loans you think you will take out in four years. How much a month will the payment be? Add $10,000 to the loan number. How much a month does that change the payment? My point in having you do this is to try and help you worry less about the money. Yes, money is a concern. But, you risk disordering your soul if you begin to worry excessively about money from a young age.

I have seen many edifying examples of families that did not worry about money, where things worked out fine. One summer, I worked with Joe. He was the second of six children. His Dad worked at WalMart. He told me stories about growing up when his Dad had was faced with paying part of the electric bill, but realizing the $50 he had would not pay the full bill, so the lights were going to be turned off anyway. To show his wife and children not to worry, the Dad said, "Okay everybody, the lights are going off tomorrow whether I send in this $50 or not, so, tonight, we are going to the movies!"

Joe's uncles and aunts often derided his parents for having six children, warning them that they would never be able to pay for their education. At the time I worked with Joe, he had just won a scholarship to go to graduate school at a respectable Southern university, his sister had a full ride to college, and her younger sister had just won a full academic scholarship to another school.

Another friend of mine, Bob, is now a very happy high school teacher in the local public high school system. He is one of eleven children and his father was a butcher. Six of the eleven children have PhDs. His Dad made between $8,000 and $16,000 a year when Bob was growing up. Bob reminded me the other day that when his mother was on her deathbed, she called Bob to the bed in order to give him her final lesson in life. When Bob came up to her, she grabbed his hand and held it hard. She pulled him close to her face, and she whispered to him, "Bob, when I was young, your father and I decided that we were not going to worry about money. The more children we had, the more people would ask us where the money would come from to feed them. We never had to worry about that. We decided that the most important thing was that we were going to be faithful to everything that the Catholic Church teaches, and that God would take care of the rest . . . . Do you got that? And when I say everything, I mean *everything!*"

So, get this worry about money out of your mind. When you are in college, you should think more about what you need to do to mature as a person than what you need to do to make yourself financially solvent. In fact one little piece of advice that might help a college student is "Do not work. Do not do work/study. Do not work in the summer to simply pass your time." I am not saying you should party the whole time either. Do not work simply to make money. If and when you work in the summer, think through why you are doing it. Again, try to do the things that will actually enable you to mature as a person.

Some people should work because that is what they need to do to mature. But if you are serious about maturing as a person there is always a way to do what will help you mature. Money is not an obstacle to maturity.

Not recognizing resources

Another common pitfall is that the students fail to realize the resources that are at their disposal. The number one resource is your friends. Maybe this is not the language to use, but you are a fool if you were to spend your time not meeting new people and making friends when you are in college. Too many students settle into a comfortable clique, which is not really a group of friends but a group of accomplices who support each other in immaturity.

Especially in your freshman year, particularly during the first semester of your freshman year, just go around the dorm and introduce yourself to people. That is a great way to meet new people. You are also a fool if you think that your friends are the people you drink with or play video games with. They are not the friends that you will remember ten or 20 years from now, if by then you have developed an upright conscience. Your friends are the people you end up having conversations with and end up drinking a glass of wine or smoking a cigar with.

There is a passage in the *Protageras* where Socrates says to Protageras, "Let us stop telling stories and interpreting stories." Let us stop being English majors. Why? Because telling stories and interpreting stories is like doing the secondary parts where nobody talks because they are playing flutes in the background all the time, to distract everybody from having a real conversation. Then Socrates says, "The good part is when you have wine and you are having a good conversation and the night flies by because you are discussing deeper things with those who are around you."

Wasting time

There are thousands of ways of wasting time.

There are many ways of turning the soul over to the pursuit of pleasure, video games, music, parties, and movies.

Video games are a huge drain on time. A student this year wrote me an apology at the end of the semester. He said that about two weeks into the class he was going to drop it because, while I was not lecturing specifically on video games, he realized that he was addicted to them, and that it was ruining his life. He had an emotional weekend in which he decided to stick with the course and try to beat this addiction. I cannot say the student beat the addiction, but I can say he was willing to admit it was a problem.

A few years back I knew another student who was coming to me for mentorship in learning how to grow in virtue. It became clear at one point that this student was not really making any friends and he was not really growing in virtue. When asked about video games, he said he played them for three to four hours a day. When asked if he could cut back a bit, he cut out. I never really saw that student again. It is easy to sit in the dorm and get excited and passionate about video games. It is easy to think that you can become one of the ranked players in the world and that that means something, or that being good at video games could help you be a pilot some day. But, it is also true that video games could become a kind of slavery. So, it would be good to set out in advance your time limits for video games, and then stick to them. Here is where a trusted advisor can be of help.

The other obvious way to waste time is going to parties. A few years back an upright student came to this realization his junior year. Reflecting on his first two years he told me that often his freshman and sophomore year he would go to parties because that is where he thought he would meet friends. Since he was not a big drinker, he did not really make any friends at the parties. Then, he realized that after the parties, he had to spend the next week scrambling to get his work done.

This student's insight is something that the better students start to realize when they are sophomores and juniors—if you go out and party too much on the weekend it destroys you for the next week; because if you do not do some work on the weekend and spend all your time either partying or recuperating from partying, then you are spending the whole week trying to catch up with your assignment. Just on the basic level of getting work done, partying is a bad idea. More importantly, you don't really make meaningful friendships at parties.

Another way to waste time is going to (or watching) movies in excess. Movies are not bad things, and we should watch them. But movies can be watched to an excess. When you are watching movies it is good to think about this possibility—for every movie I watch I should try to have a conversation about it. If I really cannot have a conversation about a movie it is probably not worth my time. Or if I could not have a conversation about the last three movies I watched, I probably need to watch movies about which I can have conversations.

Lack of planning

Another pitfall is that people do not plan out their studying. They fail to plan out assignments and how to fulfill them. The solution to this problem is simple—if you have to write a paper, start writing it as soon as you get assigned. Do not wait until the night before it's due. There are so many papers that are poorly written and the comments in the end that I write on them are simply, "If you would have just written one more draft; if it were not just your first attempt, you would have gotten a much better grade."

Avoid the pitfalls

So what do we need to do? Here are some things that can help us avoid these common pitfalls:

Start the day early

I was talking to a professor who has been here for 25 years and was himself a university undergraduate. He said, "A decisive feature and a determining factor of whether a student will really mature as a student during his four years at a university is whether or not he eats breakfast early in the morning, and before going to his first class, not in his first class."

I think he is right. I have both faith and reason to support me on this one. One of the things that Plato and Socrates would challenge their students to do at the Academy was to get up early in the morning. We also find a proverb in the Book of Wisdom that says that a just man will rise every morning early to meet his Lord (Wisdom 16:28). This is also the advice of Plato in *The Republic*. One could say it is an area where faith and reason agree.

I have noticed over the years that the students who from the very beginning start to take a more professional approach towards their studies end up being the best students. They also end up having the most fun. They end up having the most free time to spend with their friends or to take over the University or whatever else they might want to do in their four years here.

Football players have to get up sometimes early in the morning, and go do their exercises and drills. I have had football players in my class. They had to be in the weight room at six o'clock in the morning five days a week and they could not opt out of it. That's a professional approach.

Again, you are not going to see many people trying to do this. But I think it is a determining factor that if someone is going to approach their studies and their University life in a professional way they will try to live the hours of a professional man. By living the hours of a professional man they will start to reduce the number of things in their lives that could lead them into vice. Now, you might say, I know a professional man who goes and visits bars everyday after he works. Yes, that could still happen. The same man would drink more if he were unemployed. What I am speaking about here, however, is the normal professional man. This man, who has a wife and children, and who struggles to be an active participant and leader in his family, hustles to get up early, get to work, and return home so that he can spend his evenings with his family, serving each of them in the way that a father should. If you set good habits at the University, you will prepare yourself well for this task.

Put pressure on yourself

What is virtue? Virtue is a habit or a disposition to do what is good. A habit is something you do everyday, you are consistent at it. We see throughout the centuries that young students are always making excuses to stay up late, to not do their work, to put things off. One of the ways you can really use your time well is to start to develop habits by putting pressure on yourself. "Between the hours of nine and six everyday if I am not in class, I am studying or I am eating." I think that is a very good pressure to put on yourself.

Educational psychologists say that for someone to really do well in a course and retain information they have to review. After they take notes in class, sometime that day they should spend 15 minutes reviewing their notes. This increases one's capacity to remember by around 60 percent. Just the simple act of reviewing notes from that day sometime during that day will dramatically increase your capacity to remember what is going on in the class. Then once a week, take the notes from your class and review them; it will greatly increase your capacity to remember things.

I knew a student once who did this. Every day he tried to take the time to review the notes from his classes, and then he would also do this once a week on Friday afternoon at three o'clock when everybody else went out of the class to play Frisbee and what-not. If he had the time he would review his notes from the very beginning of the semester from all his classes. It was very funny to see this student because the first semester he did this, he did not have to study at all during his finals, because he knew everything. He just went around during the finals kind of making fun of it. Think of how many jokes you can pull on people during the finals if you just were to do this little exercise.

When I was in high school my dad told me this in a somewhat different way. Basically he encouraged us, his sons, to try to get our work done every day by four or five o'clock—studying for classes, reviewing notes or whatever it might be—so that in the evenings we could go play basketball, go out with our friends, be involved in a fraternity, or whatever it was. What I have found over time is that for people who do well in college there is someone who gives them some kind of advice like this and the young man follows that advice.

This summer someone told me that when he was a freshman, one of the mentors to whom he was accountable basically said, "Look, you have a choice—you can either spend your college years wasting your time, trying to have a lot of fun, going out and drinking, putting things off, doing everything at the last minute, pulling all-nighters, suffering a lot . . . or you can go to bed every night at nine thirty or ten o'clock, try to get all your work done every day by five, and have a lot more fun than everybody else." The freshman thought, "Oh how can this be?" But then his mentor was really tough on him. He would even call his mentor if he had to stay up after ten o'clock and say, "Could I stay up tonight and study?" You may laugh, but he did this. His mentor would say "O.K., 15 minutes. I give you 15 minutes." He looks back at it now and says, "You know, I got all my work done, I never pulled an all-nighter, and I had lot more fun than a lot of my friends. I too had a very demanding schedule but I did much more than they did."

So it is hard, but it is possible.

Schedule your time

It is very important to have a schedule. There are two things that I am going to give you as homework for this chapter. One is just to fill out a schedule what you are going to be doing each day. The other is to fill out a schedule of what you *could* do each day.

This is tough, but it is not so that I can hammer you. It is to discover whether you are suffering like the freshman while he was putting things off and messing things up, or whether you have arrived at the point where he was after his mentor was tough on him.

Avoid late nights

Avoid the late-night parties. Go out on Friday and Saturday night, but make a resolution something to the effect of: at midnight I am leaving.

My family owned five bars growing up so I know the alcohol culture. One of my first memories in life is of this drunk. He was a truck driver trying to explain the meaning of life to me. I was around eight years old. He stood there slurring his words; I do not even remember what he said. I was an eight-year-old, so give me a break. But I just remember he was really sad. Poor guy.

Most people, after the second drink, are not going to remember much about what they said anyway. So in some sense a rule of thumb to follow at parties is when you notice that most people have had their second drink it is time to go. That is usually around midnight. Maybe it is earlier, depending on how hard they are drinking.

But I think it is good to think of it this way: If I go to bed at midnight or 1 A.M., and wake up at 8 or 9 A.M. during the weekend, I get up at a quiet time when most people are sleeping. Go down to the study room, and you can get a lot of studying, reading, or writing done in a very common peaceful way. And then everybody else gets up and the day starts.

People realize this generally when they are in their sophomore or junior year, especially given football games in the Fall and things like that. If you do not try to use some time on a weekend to study and do work, you will always be playing catch up. You will always have this sense that you are behind, scrambling each week to finish assignments at the last minute and pull all-nighters to finish projects and prepare for tests.

There was another student who would eat his breakfast every Saturday at 6:45 A.M. He would go find a room in a classroom building and he would study there until game time. He would go to the game, and have a great time. After the game, he would go back to his classroom, study there until late at night, and Saturday night he would watch a movie or go out with his friends. He says that is the thing that helped him survive through college. During the week he got busy with activities, dealing with people and the like. Saturdays were his savior as far as being able to stay up on things.

Summary

Obviously the culture is pushing you in a direction of being a permanent adolescent, of never growing up. Of remaining a perpetual adolescent consuming what other people tell them to buy and to think. There is nothing you can do about that right now, except choose the path of virtue, and find the resources to grow in this path.

There are lots of resources that are at your disposal at the University—professors, research opportunities, internships. You can even get money from the University to travel abroad in the summers. What I would like to do over the next couple of weeks is to go over more of these different aspects of how you can use your years at the University. The big thing about this week is thinking about schedule—scheduling your time.

Looking ahead

So make a schedule and fill in how you would like to spend each hour of the day. Then, challenge yourself to stick to it. Sometimes, to start out, you have to simply write down how you actually spend your time each day. It can be very helpful to spend a day or two just writing down how you spend your time. Then, on your own or with someone's help, make a new schedule of what you *could* do; of how you hope to challenge yourself to spend your time better. Before moving on, you can easily use a computer program to recreate and fill out something like the sample schedule at the end of this chapter.

Time	Monday	Tuesday	Wed	Thurs	Friday	Saturday	Sunday
7							
7:30							
8							
8:30							
9							
9:30							
10							
10:30							
11							
11:30							
12							
12:30							
1							
1:30							
2							
2:30							
3							
3:30							
4							
4:30							
5							
5:30							
6							
6:30							
7							
7:30							
8							
8:30							
9							
9:30							
10							

JEFFREY J. LANGAN

CHAPTER FOUR

" WITHOUT JESUS CHRIST, man must be in vice and misery; with Jesus Christ, man is freed from vice and misery. In him are all our virtue and all our bliss; outside him there are only vice, misery, errors, darkness, death, and despair." Pascal, *Penseés* 546

Now the works of the flesh are plain: fornication, impurity, licentiousness, idolatry, sorcery, enmity, strife, jealousy, anger, selfishness, dissension, party spirit, envy, drunkenness, carousing, and the like. I warn you, as I warned you before, that those who do such things shall not inherit the kingdom of God. Galatians 5: 19-21

Our current environment

In the *Alcibiades II*, Alcibiades receives some of his first practical lessons from Socrates. These lessons are meant to help Alcibiades begin to acquire virtue so that he can then begin to train his intellect. In a move that is perhaps not familiar to contemporary sensibilities, one of the first things that Socrates teaches Alcibiades is how to communicate or meditate on the Divine Being. Translating this into modern idiom, we could say that the first way we start to grow in virtue is by prayer. In *The Republic* Socrates seems to teach a similar lesson to Glaucon and Adeimantus. We grow in virtue by getting up early in the morning and speaking to God. Then, we make demands on ourselves as far as our classes.

I think in our terms in the University we should try to take classes with the Professors who will make demands on us. There is the temptation in universities to always take the easy way out. We all know Professors who have the reputation for being easier—the easy A.

We should try to acquire an education that helps us to be brutally sincere about the facts of our civilization, and about the facts of our own souls. But to evaluate society, you first have to learn how to evaluate or examine yourself. The only way to really start to grow in virtue is to be brutally sincere about who you are. This is where spiritual direction, confession or having a mentor of some sort to whom you are brutally sincere about yourself and who helps you to be brutally sincere about yourself, comes in. It is very hard to speak to another human being in a truthful way about who you are, along with dispositions to change for the better, but it is also very good. So it would be good for you to write down what your actual schedule is, put down what you actually do each day and find a mentor and then say to that person, "this is what I do each day," with the dispositions to receive, interiorize, and put into practice the advice that you hear.

If we can be honest demanding with ourselves in our efforts to grow in virtue, we can then be brutally honest about the environment we find ourselves in.

One Fall, some alumni of a Christian university here organized a meeting between a few professors and some students, the purpose being to assess the identity of what had become a modern research university with goals antithetical to Christian identity. One professor who had been at the university a long time was very forthright. He said, "Look, we have to admit the brutal facts about our situation. At a typical Catholic university with 800 faculty members, you may have between 40 and 60 that are truly concerned about Catholic identity. At the same time, a typical research university might have 2,000 or 3,000 faculty. A handful of them, maybe ten to 20, are concerned about preserving Western civilization in any kind of serious way. Most professors do not think about it one way or the other. They just do their job, whatever that is. But then there is also a large element that is working actively to undo the good and the salutary customs and institutions, like the family, that are an integral part not just of Western civilization, but of any culture."

The professor said in a matter-of-fact way, "We live in an age of decadence, an age where our educators, whether at secular or at Catholic Universities often themselves are unaware of the basic principles of the moral order. Many professors have the equivalent of a grade school understanding of the Catholic faith, or have never studied in a serious way the principles of the moral order. They were once students much like you, who adopted one moral position or another without much reflection. At the same time, many do not see much of a relationship between their field of study and the moral order itself. This very way of seeing themselves is the result of specific philosophical positions taken 200 years ago. That is, the professors are not aware of the principles and the history that have formed them to think of themselves as they do."

Why did he say that? He said that because the family is crumbling. He said that because we live in a society where people give more importance to money and comfort than to any other standard of behavior. Their children give more importance to pleasure-seeking and narcotics and whatever their desires suggest to them. In that kind of a culture we also then have the problem of power-seeking. When the family breaks down and licentiousness becomes rampant, the next stage is power-seeking, or empire-building, or something of a similar nature.

Plato's response to this (and that of Socrates as well) when he saw this happening to Athens in the fifth century B.C. was to say, "The problem with all these supposed great leaders of Athens and of Greece is that they failed to teach people, failed to establish customs; they failed to teach their children virtue." While the fathers were out fighting wars, expanding economic markets and opportunities, and gaining money for living comfortable lives, they neglected instructing their children in virtue. Their children became intemperate and instead of living happy lives, they sought happiness in money, pleasure or power.

You can look at the modern West, especially in the last 200 years, and you can almost see it regressing morally in the same way that Plato saw Athens degenerating from the high standard of moral virtue it upheld during the fourth century B.C.

Moral training

Socrates was the first person to discover and articulate what virtue is. Virtue involves developing the powers of the soul. Specifically, virtue is developing habits or dispositions in your soul to lead you to do what is good and to avoid what is evil. Socrates developed both the moral and the intellectual training that would help someone acquire virtue. How do you train someone to have good habits—is it by teaching them to chop heads off? The answer is no. There is something more involved. The first thing that Socrates would teach his students to do was to pray.

In *Alcibiades* I, Socrates teaches Alcibiades what it means to start to care for his soul. Socrates met Alcibiades at the moment when the 18-year-old Alcibiades was on his way to the legislature to convince Athens to declare war on Sparta. Alcibiades thought that such a war would be a chance for him to win glory for himself and Athens. Socrates convinced Alcibiades, at least for the moment, to put off war making, learning how to chop off heads, and to instead cultivate virtues in his soul. Then, Socrates teaches Alcibiades that if he wants to develop virtue in his soul, he needs to first learn how to contemplate the divine. Socrates says, "If you want to be a leader, the most important thing is not to figure out how to get yourself into a position of power. If you want to be a leader, the most important thing is to start to learn how to shape your soul and to do that, you need to look at your soul from the point of view of God, whom you should befriend."

A more contemporary example illustrates the same point. During the Second Vatican Council, a group of cardinals had dinner with St. Josemaria Escrivá in order to discuss the role of ordinary women and men in transforming society according to spiritual principles. In the middle of this conversation, one of the cardinals said it was going to be laywomen and men who in the next 100 or 200 years will be responsible for Christianizing society. They have to do it. St. Josemaria interrupted the cardinal, effectively saying that it would not simply be the laymen who were going to be responsible for society. The laymen would have to first learn how to pray, or how to become contemplative souls. Why? If they did not have souls of prayer, then, when they went into society, rather than transforming it according to the order that is in their souls, they would either get sucked up by that society and adopt its unchristian customs (and in some sense be figuratively eaten alive), or they would so compromise their faith in order to get access to "important" jobs and professions that they would simply project the disorder that is in their souls onto society (Andrés Vázquez de Prada, *The Founder of Opus Dei, Volume III*, 2002, 340, esp. fn 77).

The moral of the story is, if you want to change society and make it harmonize better with the moral order in things, the first thing you have to do is learn how to order your soul. If you want to order your soul, you have to become friends with God, so that He can teach you and help you order your soul. If you fail to order your soul, you will project disorder from your soul into the world.

The first Christians

What really matters for the goal of being a cultural leader is becoming someone whose soul is properly ordered. St. Alphonsus Ligouri wrote *The Victories of the Martyrs*. Theologians have always recognized that the great witnesses of Christianity were the first Christians from the first century until the fifth or sixth century in Rome. They were fervent and had incredibly ordered souls. They would not back down on anything of importance to the faith. They would rather die than back down. And so, they gave witness to the truth of morality, sometimes to the point of dying rather than being forced to commit an offense against God.

I recommend everybody read the English translation of *Victories of the Martyrs*. The story of St. Catherine of Alexandria is an excellent and typical example. As a teenage girl, she became acquainted with the Gospels. She also became convinced that the Gospels contained within them a wisdom that was greater than the wisdom of the philosophers. She took her convictions with her to the academies and schools of Alexandria, challenging the philosophers with her newfound sublime wisdom. When the Emperor came through Alexandria, she did not fear standing in front of his chariot to remind him of the unjust policies that he empire had dictated against the Christians. Her actions cost her her life, but they also were one of many of the acts of fortitude displayed by the early Christians in winning over the Roman Empire.

The story of St. Catherine is typical of the stories of the martyrs and they all remind us of the kind of fortitude required to preserve ourselves and to expand the regime of virtue. What you will realize if you read *The Victories of the Martyrs* is that when these martyrs were marching off to their death or when they got pulled in front of the judges or courts they would say, "I am happy. First of all I refuse to sin in any way. The last thing I would want to do is offend God. Second, I am happy to die if you are going to put me to death for not offending God." And they were proud. They felt they had won a crown, a victory, if they died rather than offend God.

If they could die rather than offend God, why do theologians say that the martyrs were the great tributes and the great proof of the Christian faith? First, because it was true; second, they were so convinced, not just intellectually but morally, that it was true that their faith filtered down to every little detail of their lives.

We sometimes tend to be people who think we know the truth intellectually, but we fail to let the truth filter down to every detail of our lives. Maybe we miss out on the fact that education is not simply intellectual training. Education is also moral training and developing habits. Virtues are the fruit of the habits that we develop. Ultimately, the martyrs had the supernatural virtues and so over time they created a culture, which was a Christian culture with Christian customs and Christian habits. They rejected a culture which was pagan, with customs and traditions hostile to the Christian way of life. Over the past 200 years, we in the West have re-incorporated in a mass way the anti-Christian way of life. Unfortunately, many have remained Christian while still embracing pagan customs and habits.

The war against the Christian way of life

To give a radical example of the difference between the Christian way of life and the pagan way of life, I offer you the example of St. John Chrysostom. St. John Chrysostom said, "We Christians do not live like the pagans who mix the sexes together at every opportunity. We Christians live a seemly separation of the sexes." Because it helps us to live with modesty, chastity, purity—so that we can love God alone. It is not that men never deal with women and vice versa, but we Christians live a seemly separation of the sexes. These customs and institutions remained more or less in place for a long time.

What is implied in this statement is that the non-Christians or the pre-Christians did not live a seemly separation of the sexes. That was a society in which men exercised power over women, dominated them, and mixed them into religious worship for the sake of the orgies that were often associated with the pagan rituals. The seemly separation of the sexes was designed to prevent this kind of behavior. It was not for the purpose of discriminating against one sex or the other. Inasmuch as our culture has re-adopted pagan ways, it has stopped living this Christian seemly separation of the sexes.

The first signs of a kind of open warfare against Christian customs and institutions in the West took place in the Albigenisian crisis of the 11th and 12th centuries. That revolution did not sustain itself. The next open revolution against Christian customs and culture took place during the Hussite revolution in the Czech Republic in 1410. It is one of the ironies of history that the fall of Rome is earmarked as 410 A.D. The Hussite revolution began in 1410.

JEFFREY J. LANGAN

Between these two dates, we have a 1,000-year rule of Christianity. The Hussite revolution was able to sustain itself. It was able to grow into what we now call the Protestant revolution.

Nietzsche said that Huss and Luther started what he was bringing to full completion—a kind of assertion of the human will against the authority that builds up virtue.

The Reformation gave birth to the modern nation state. The modern nation state precisely tries to separate Christians from their faith, so that they worship the nation rather than their faith, follow their Church or love their God. That gives rise to all the revolutionary ideologies of the 20th century such as materialistic capitalism. For a 60-year period in the 20th century there was a revolt against materialistic capitalism in the form of fascism and communism. We are now returning to the times of materialistic capitalism. All these are political and cultural forms of rebellion against the Christian moral order.

The Christian customs and institutions that the first Christians established in a hostile environment—remember they were visitors; they were not the home team in the Roman Empire—more or less stayed in place until probably the 19th century. By the 19th century the 500-year war against Christianity began to bear fruit—in civilizational ways. By the 20th century most Christian customs and Christian institutions had become weakened.

Christian culture today

Catholics and Christians for the most part are on the run all around the world. Catholics are weak and divided. They are living lives in which they are mostly seeking either comfort or pleasure. They tend to be dominated by the ruling class, which by and large rules according to some sort of modern capitalist ideology, sexual liberationist ideology or some sort of ideology which is hostile to Christian institutions, values and customs. Many Catholics have simply adopted the morality of their oppressors.

Oftentimes in capitalist countries, Catholics pride themselves on being capitalist or being members of political parties which promote that ideology. In other ways, Catholics will pride themselves on being feminists or sexual liberationists.

I include America in this list. People have deviated in so many different ways that it is easy to avoid looking at our own internal disorders. We can always point to somebody else and say, "I am not as bad as that guy." The capitalists point at the sexual liberationists and say, "At least I am not as bad as those people who are getting abortions." The pacifists point at the capitalists and say, "At least I am not a capitalist Catholic who is grinding the poor to dust." Both can point to the warmongers, and say, "At least I am not a bloodthirsty empire builder." We can point at people who are getting drunk all the time, or who are having orgies and all sorts of crazy parties and we can say, "At least I am not as bad as those guys."

The problem is that this was not the attitude of the first Christians, and the modern attitude, if not corrected, will stunt our own growth in virtue. The first Christians would not look around and say, "I am not as bad as that guy." The first Christians would say, "I am not as good as Christ. He is the model who I have to stand up to. Somehow I have to struggle to shape my soul to make it more like Christ. I have to shape my soul to be more like the soul of Christ, so that when I am working, whether it is in the army, or in my shop, or wherever I work, I am projecting Christ into the institutions where I am working."

Politaea

Another approach to this idea comes from understanding the title of Plato's great piece of moral philosophy, *The Republic* (Trans. by Allan Bloom, 1968, 439-440, fn. 1). We need to understand what "republic" means. The Greek title of *The Republic* is *Politaea*. When you read an edition of *The Republic* that has good footnotes, you should try to read them. They will teach you something. But what does *Politaea* mean? The translator of one edition says, "It is the community of men sharing a way of life and governing themselves; it is people sharing a way of life and governing themselves—waging war and preserving the peace. It is the natural social group."

Politaea is not the state in the modern sense. Sharing a way of life means that we try to have the same habits, the same dispositions; we try to think the same about similar things. Our notion of state does not fully capture what *Polis* means.

JEFFREY J. LANGAN

Moreover, in Bloom's edition, towards the bottom of page 439, he says it should be borne in mind that words like "Statesman" and "Citizen" are based on the word *Polis*. A Statesman is the person who protects the life of the people. A Citizen is one who follows the Statesman and somehow also sees himself as working with the Statesman to preserve the way of life of those people. A Citizen is one who belongs to the city and the Statesman is one who knows all the institutions that make up a city as well as the general principles which women and men should follow in order to become happy. The Statesman knows the proper order of the human soul and role of various institutions of society—the business institutions, the military, politics, laws, courts, and the media and entertainment industries; he knows the effects that these institutions have on individual souls. The Statesman knows what the common good is, as does the Citizen, and the two, in any *Politaea,* are working together to bring it about.

Politics is merely what has to do with a city. Even in the Greek terminology between citizen, city and politics there is unity of thought; the words are similar. The footnote continues, "The Polis is given its character and its peculiar way of life is established by the organization of the city's diverse elements."

I think our notion of "common good" is closer to what Plato means when he says *Politaea.*

The common good

The **common good** is that which enables individuals, groups and the community as a whole to flourish. It is a sign of the individuals, the groups and the unity of the whole flourishing. The common good is all of the things of the city or all of the things of a group woven together to harmoniously function together. The central political concern is the proper organization of a city—who should do what job and so on. The *Politaea* is that organization.

If you think about it, the hierarchy of the Church is a good example of a *Politaea*. There are different functions in the Church. There are laymen, priests, religious bishops, archbishops, cardinals, and the Pope.

Returning to Bloom's footnote in the *Republic*, it says, "The Politaea can largely be identified with the class of citizens who rule. What is most important in a city, what is most important for protecting a way of life is to look at those who rule, to look at the leaders." If you remember from a previous chapter, the leaders can be found in particular institutions in society.

I do not mean that that these groups should assert themselves to be leaders. It is almost like a sociological fact that these are the leaders. Football players are leaders on many University campuses not by the fact that they assert themselves to be leaders, but instead by the fact that so many look to them as representing the University, and many, in turn, will imitate or actually do what the players do. One player gets a Mohawk and students start imitating his Mohawk. It is a silly thing but it is a sign. People look to leaders to set an example. It is almost a subconscious thing.

As a teacher I know that every classroom has leaders among the students. Without realizing it, the students are always looking for who the leaders are. Then they behave according to the signals that the leaders give out. If the leaders are with you as a teacher, the whole class is with you. If the leaders go against you, then the whole class goes against you, the teacher.

The souls of the leaders

If you really want to understand the character of a community, or of a city, or of a country, you look to and study the souls of the leaders. Over time, the souls of the leaders will be projected into the institutions that make up society. This is not by power-mongering or coercion or force, but gradually it is a sociological fact—the leaders will project their way of life into the institutions that they are heading, and the institutions, in turn, will form the laws and customs. The institutions, laws and customs together form the citizens. The leaders and the institutions combined will form the citizens.

So the *Politaea* can largely be identified with the class of citizens who rule. The leaders impress their way on the city and are the source of the laws. They impress their ways on the city the way that a football player impresses on people the desire to have a Mohawk. Because he does it, they want to do it.

The leaders will also project into the laws their vision of what a human is and what a community is. The leaders have authority, which is distinct from power. Because of this authority, they tend to set the standards by which citizens judge their behavior to be good or evil. They inform the customs and laws, which, in turn shape the souls of the citizens through education. Leaders, the customs, the laws and education have a huge influence on the structure and the mentality of a society. They influence the basic opinions and dispositions of people over time. By knowing the souls of the leaders, an attentive observer could guess with a certain probability about the overall direction and future of that society. When we study a society, we can look to the souls of the leaders in order to understand a significant variable that helps us understand the overall direction that that society will take in its public life over time.

Standards set by leaders

If all the leaders are committed to making money, that standard is going to become the standard that gets impregnated into the laws and institutions of society. This happens independently of Alan Greenspan's interest rate adjustments in any given year and what people think about it. The fact is that the standard for money-making will become the standard by which people are judging their behavior.

The same thing is true with respect to foreign policy. If we start to develop a Machiavellian foreign policy in which we are playing by Machiavellian rules—to gain power for the American empire, to spread it around the world—that will happen because power, or self-interest, is going to become the standard of our behavior. This happens independently of what anyone's view might be towards what the president is doing in any given moment. Gaining power becomes the standard because our souls have become such that we no longer are concerned about virtue, justice, prudence, temperance or wisdom. These are not the standards by which we are judging our behavior and our leadership positions anymore. We are judging the standard of what is good or bad by whether we advance or regress in our power.

Even in disagreements that exist between parties the basic disagreement these days is not justice but power. Policy thinkers tend to disagree about how the U.S. should project its power in the world. The standard of judgment is what is the self-interest of the United States, not what is just. And so, in foreign policy, power as a standard has replaced virtue as a standard in judging American actions abroad. This is true both of the Democrats and the Republicans. A challenge for a young woman or man interested in international affairs would be to understand the criteria of justice and prudence as taught over the centuries in Catholic Social Teaching, in order to assess or make foreign policy that is consistent with the principles of justice. At the same time, it would be very fruitful and beneficial for the common good if economists and politicians were to also attempt to create domestic economic policy in a way that harmonizes the requirements of the common good as articulated by the principles of Catholic Social Teaching over the centuries. Rather than a fruitless or naïve task, this approach is the one that will most help us address the international and domestic problems that we face.

What is interesting about this discussion is that all of our political leaders, whether they are on the "right" or the "left," seem to use the standard of power, and not the standard of virtue for judging behavior. So in that sense this is an example of what Plato means when he says, "They are going to project their souls into the institutions." Their souls are basically souls that use power or success, not justice or virtue, as the standard for judging behavior.

If you want to know what a city is like, look to the leaders because they impress their ways upon the city. The way of life of the leaders becomes the way of life of everybody else, almost by osmosis. They are also the source for the laws, the rationale for the laws—how people justify the laws. And so Bloom reminds us that "The *Politaea* is as it were the soul of the city."

The body is the matter; the soul is the form. The individuals, their families, the different trade unions, the groups, the different jobs or professions you could have in the city—these compose the matter or body of the city. The soul of the city is *Politaea*, the ordering of the soul of the leaders.

The *Politaea* is related to the individuals who compose the city as form is to matter. The soul is the form of the body. *Politaea* is the form of the city. The best English term for *politaea* is *regime*. The book which describes the best political life is appropriately entitled "The Regime."

"Such an approach to the political problem is characteristically platonic. Any attempt to recover the Greek understanding of human things requires a consideration of the sense in which *Politaea* is the single most important political fact and the cause of man's characters and ways of life." This is the point here: to understand why men live the way they live and what is the way of life of a particular society, we look to the souls of the leaders. What

JEFFREY J. LANGAN

is the standard by which they judge their behavior, what is the standard by which they live their lives?

Ultimately, Socrates argues that those who could be leaders should not be concerned about becoming powerful, they should not be concerned about what they need to do to get the right job or to get in the right position in society. Obviously, they have to do something in life, they have to get jobs and work in all parts of society but their primary concern should be how to order their souls, not to gain positions so as to exercise power.

Analyzing the character of the soul

The Republic is not a public policy proposal although probably 90 percent of the scholars will read it as such. They err in doing so. *The Republic* is an attempt to analyze the character of the soul. What is the character of the soul inasmuch as it can influence the community? The purpose of *The Republic* is to ask, "What is the form of political society?"

Plato gives crazy and bizarre examples in *The Republic* because, basically, he is trying to help us create the image in our mind of what the form is. In Book V, for example, when he says that the city should have all the women and children in common, he is setting up an analogy for the soul. The children are the ideas that the soul produces. The women are the rational part of the soul. He does not think that a society could ever actually hold all the women and children in common, although many readers of Plato over the years have assumed that this is what he was advocating. However, Plato was attempting to provide us with a radical image of the parts of the soul. Socrates with him will argue that a true leader shapes his soul. This is the purpose of the crazy examples that you will see in Book V of the *Republic*.

A true leader shapes his soul. This is why it might be helpful for you to make out a time-line on a sheet of paper. If you did not do so earlier, now might be a time to make one. If you did draw one earlier, it might be worthwhile to ask yourself if there are some things on your line you want to change. Draw a line. Write down the current year at the left end of the line. Moving to the right, every inch or so, write down the year it will be in ten years, and your age in ten years underneath. Probably around 30 you can write down marriage (though if you should be married I would suggest sooner), around 50 or so you will be a grandparent, and around 65 you will retire. At some point, around 80, write death. It can be helpful and interesting to then write down what you think you want to be or do at each of these ages.

By the end of *The Republic*, the people who were arguing with Plato at one point effectively say, "Socrates we agree with what you want to do. But it seems as if this is impossible." And Socrates corrects them, "What I am proposing is admittedly difficult but it is not impossible." They say "Then, what can we do?" Socrates replies, "Well, first you have to gather together in a small group and start challenging each other to get up early in the morning, to make demands on each other. In other words, start to demand of each other that you grow in virtue. You should take a demanding set of classes." That last utterance is, of course, a translation into modern lingo. But it makes the point that if the transformation of society along the lines of virtue is going to take place, it will do so only if there are groups of students and citizens of all kinds who start to specifically challenge each other to grow in virtue.

CHAPTER FIVE

" THIS INNER WAR of reason against the passions has resulted in a division into two sects among those who have sought to find peace. Some have endeavored to renounce the passions to become gods; others have endeavored to renounce reason and become mere brutes." Pascal, *Penseés* 413

Deconstructivist Thought

As we read in Chapter 3, in the *Protagoras* Socrates says, "We should stop talking about what our different interpretations are of the things that we are reading. That is similar to going to a second rate drinking party where everybody is drinking just to get drunk. They have music playing in the background, so that they cannot talk to each other, and they just get drunk. A first-rate drinking party would be one where the alcohol that you have is just to loosen you up a little bit so you can have a good conversation and get to the truth of things."

Great Books Programs

Someone might wonder whether simply reading the Great Books is a way to ensure that students learn the truth, the good, and how to live virtue. I do not think that this necessarily the case. Almost all students I know, especially men, tend to be like the people at a poorly organized drinking party. This is true especially of business majors, including those who participate in Great Books programs—especially Great Books programs, because these programs if poorly organized encourage weak and lazy thinking more so than almost any other major. Great Bookies talk about all the different ways of interpreting things, without ever getting to the truth of things.

The ideal of teaching the Great Books was that the professor would help the students learn how to argue so that they can arrive at the truth of things. You need the professor there—to set the standards of argument. What has happened in a typical Great Books program is a tragic regression. Several programs started with teaching the Classics of Western Civilization. They taught Homer, Plato, Virgil, Shakespeare, and the best authors of each discipline. But, usually, such programs lose their initial fervor. First, the professors became doubtful about the possibility of arriving at the truth. Then, the professor was no longer seen as someone who was helping the students learn how to argue so as to arrive at the truth of things. The professor became a moderator of the discussion. Next, the leaders of the programs decided that instead of teaching the great books, teachers would teach the Great Books of their specialties. Before long, there is little difference between a Great Books program and any other university program, especially with respect to pursuing and living the truth.

Typically all the various students just propose their alternative interpretations. Nobody learns the criteria of argument—how we go from a situation of apparent relativism to arrive at the knowledge of the truth of things. The truth is not in the text; the truth is in the reality. The text is something that helps you understand reality.

Most people who truly want to learn how to argue get disenchanted with their Great Books program and pick up a second major which helps them to learn how to argue. Learning how to argue does not mean to point fingers at people and get mad. To argue is to go from what is more known to what is less known in a rational way such that both parties arguing can arrive at the truth of things. Or they acquire a major, such as history, in which professors who are knowledgeable can help the students acquire a context within which to understand and assess the evidence used in order to write the story of the human race.

In a modern university, the deconstruction of the text is all that we have to go on, but there is no ultimate meaning in the text. In other words, the text does not mean anything. The text means whatever you want it to mean. Each person can elicit or make his or her own meaning from the text. If there is no truth that the text points to, then interpretation of the text will become a power game. Whoever is the cleverest at establishing power will be able to impose his interpretation on the rest of the discipline. In modern academia, this is done by controlling who gets into graduate school, who gets hired, who gets money from foundations and the University administration, and who gets tenure. These are the mechanisms of power and control.

Ironically, in the face of a lack of truth, in a situation where we have deconstructionism, there are many similarities between the ways English professors deal with texts and the relativistic way that Imams deal with the Koran or Rabbis deal with the Talmud. That is, you can only get out of the text what the Rabbi or the professor allows you to get out of it. In other words, power rules. The person who has power is the one who determines the meaning of the text. There is, in all these systems, no truth outside of the text by which we can judge whether the text is accurate, true, or false.

Most literary interpretation has gone the way of deconstructionism since the 1950s. Most English courses will be taught that way. My guess is that the vast majority—probably 60 or 70 percent—of the seminar courses, will be taught that way.

When education becomes deconstructionist, students will become weak and lazy in their thinking. If you can propose anything as being legitimate, then there is no standard or criterion by which a teacher can challenge you to be better.

I once attended a depressing lecture by a Canadian professor at the University of Toronto. The professor said, "When I was going to school in the 1950s there were all these great books programs and the professors were trying to convince us that there was really nothing great about the books we were reading. They were not pointing us to any truth. When I first became a professor in the 1970s, everybody was changing the great books from the great classics to whatever the professors thought were the great books. Later, the students of those professors in the 1980s and 1990s became deconstructionists and began convincing students that there were really no great books in any one discipline. Now students just do not want to read." At the end of the lecture I felt, "Yes, he got it!" Everybody else was depressed though. They felt, "Oh, what are we doing?"

We went from reading great books to reading books that the professors thought were great (but were not in fact great), to reading great books as a discipline, to students not wanting to read. There was a regression similar to reading SparkNotes on the Internet instead of reading the actual book.

Our culture tends towards activity and away from learning. So, as long as we just talk about things we will tend not to read. Our culture also tends towards relativism, so as long as we lack a scientific approach, we will tend to become lazy thinkers. Unfortunately, great books programs, as with all other academic programs, if not vigilantly maintained, will degrade into programs that subvert virtue rather than promote it.

When an educational culture becomes success-oriented and oligarchic, people will try to give the appearance of knowing something so that they can achieve success even though they do not really know that thing. They have the appearance of knowledge but not true knowledge.

If you are in a relativistic or deconstructionist environment why not just have the appearance of knowledge instead of true knowledge? What is the difference? Therefore, deconstructionism will foster laziness, poor argumentation and vice among the students. As professors become deconstructionists and relativists and existentialists, Universities become corrupt. The behavior of the students becomes corrupt.

We are human; we have original sin. We are always going to be prone to corrupt things. The question is whether the institution gives us more rather than fewer rationalizations for doing the corrupt things that we are doing. Departments and Universities that should be encouraging enquiry into timeless truths and principles and helping students to build up the moral life that began with what their parents started in grade school and high school. When departments and Universities stop doing that job and start teaching false ideas they will basically start to provide the students with rationalizations that lead them away from the moral order. They will help the students rationalize behavior that will do damage to their souls and damage to society over time.

This is not the first generation in the history of the world in which students rebelled against authority. The difference is that the relativistic ideas that the professors are teaching, which are an ideology, are further exacerbating the problem. They are further confirming the students in their efforts to pursue lust and rebellion against authority.

This ideology is becoming the prejudice of our age.

The Apology of Socrates

These prejudices show themselves in the typical way that students see *The Apology* of Socrates. When I have students write about *The Apology*, they say Socrates was a great man. He should not have been put to death because he just went against what his society wanted him to do. And, they say, that is not a bad thing.

However, that is not what Socrates was doing. Socrates was put to death by the Sophists, who were relativists. The Sophists were the ones that said there was no truth. They were the ones that said that society is governed by power relationships. The Sophists were the ones that were trying to encourage the youth of Athens to eat, drink and be merry because tomorrow you might die. And Socrates upset these people. He angered them because he said that there is a truth that we can know and we can shape our souls to learn how to approach the truth. That is why he was put to death. It is not because he went against the values of the society at the time.

But we are so conditioned that when we read *The Apology* for the first time, this is the interpretation that immediately forces itself into our minds. We think we are being unique and creative, but everybody says the same thing. If you talk to professors about *The Apology*, most of them would just gloss over the truth and relativism question and just let every student completely misinterpret *The Apology*.

You may think, "The Sophists obviously had some degree of power. They were encouraging citizens to acquire power and telling them everything was relative. Socrates was basically saying the opposite things. Was he not rebelling against society?" This is true in a way but not in the way that you are thinking.

We are taught to think that rebellion against the authority is rebelling against your parents, rebelling against the Church and rebelling against any institution that can pretend to teach justice and virtue. However, the kind of authority that Socrates is rebelling against is the authority that establishes itself on power, or authority that establishes itself by getting you to follow your passions. I would agree with you on that point. But, there is a difference between a young man becoming subversive—to commit himself to promoting licentiousness by doing impure things and trying to encourage others to do the same—and a young man, like one of the first Christians, who rebels against a licentious culture by not doing what is unjust. The second is the only real form of rebellion, it is God's rebellion. The first is an illegitimate rebellion, or a rebellion that is predicated on a lie.

But when a student says Socrates was going against the values of his society, what is going through his mind is that society is somehow the Church. And the Church is this stodgy, monolithic, authoritarian institution. And anyone who goes against it is good. Anybody who supports it is bad or evil. These are the prejudices of modern times.

Somehow, the myth—which by the way rose from the Cabbala which arose in the 12th century—is that the only way we can truly be free is if we do evil. If we rebel against the Church and we do evil, then we really know and we are free. This is sometimes the false promise of modern science. That is what Cabbala taught. It became popular in Western Europe by the 13th and 14th centuries.

So in a sense the critique about rebellion is right. But that is not what people mean when they say what they say about *The Apology*. And God's rebellion has nothing in common with the crass, vulgar way in which deconstructionism is applied is by the business major or by the anthropology major or the ultimate Frisbee house or the fraternities. Basically, they use rationalizations as a justification for expanding the power of capitalism, empire building or the more simple vulgarities like doing narcotics, having orgies, and such. In short, they are advocating a return to paganism. They institutionalize and maintain an adolescent, almost pre-pubescent, rebellion against authority that prevents souls from maturing. They understand authority to be this monolithic Church which is trying to oppress everybody.

Socrates was not rebelling in the adolescent way. He was against rebellion. He would not go against the laws of Athens. A rebel will try to undermine the laws—Socrates was not willing to do that. He was a rebel for the truth.

In the *Dialogues*, it is always Socrates and a small group, because he did not like large groups. He thought that by their very nature the people who are trying to have a debate in front of a large group will try to be sophistical and appeal to the passions of the group rather than to arrive at the truth of the thing. So he always resisted arguing in front of large groups.

The people who opposed Socrates

The people who, by their own admission, hated sophistical ideas aligned themselves for some reason with the sophists in order to put Socrates to death. The sophists had somehow tricked enough normal Athenian citizens to go along with them in the trial.

Not long after the trial, the Athenian citizens realized that they had been tricked by the sophists and that they had put a just man to death, and they stoned a number of the sophists to death. Any society at any given time can become blind to the injustice that she does. At some point though, she will wake up and realize, "Oh my gosh, why did I just trust this person?"

This is what happened at the trial and death of Socrates. The people and the jury turned around and stoned the leaders of the jury to death—the people even stoned the sophists.

A barbaric approach to life

I have an example that suggests the intellectual and moral character of the people who opposed Socrates. It is the story of a student who was an applicant for the Rhodes Scholarship, an adjunct professor who was a Christian philosopher, and an old man who was a graduate of the same University where the student attended classes and where the adjunct taught. The three also lived in the same neighborhood and belonged to the same neighborhood association.

The Rhodes Scholarship is an annual scholarship that the top seniors apply for, in the hopes that they will get to study in England for one to three years. It was set up by Cecil Rhodes in the last century as a way of fostering intellectual and cultural ties between England and her former colonies, including the United States. It is now one of the most prestigious scholarships students can obtain.

These three men used to sit in neighborhood association meetings in which the association had to discuss how to deal with the students living in the neighborhood. The people from the neighborhood association were simple Joe and Jane Six-Packs. They could care less about students, their lifestyles, or the mostly subversive ideas they learn at the University. Yet, over the course of three or four months the neighborhood association in general, and this old man in particular, took a liking to the Rhodes applicant simply because he was a Rhodes applicant.

A year before, during some meetings, this same old man had befriended a Marxist student and jeered at the adjunct Christian philosopher every time he met him. This was because he had heard a rumor about that philosopher, and the kind of philosophy he taught. The old man had heard that Christian philosophers were too "traditionalist" in their approach, and that, therefore, they had no place in a modern research University. Every time the old man saw the adjunct he would sneer at him, and attribute Machiavellian motives to all his dealings. The old man detested the adjunct. He did all he could do to treat the adjunct rudely. And yet, this old man has much more in common with the adjunct from a philosophical standpoint than he did with the potential Rhodes Scholar applicant.

The Rhodes Scholar applicant had to do something to make himself famous in order to win the Rhodes scholarship. So, he organized a march in the city to raise awareness about problems in Uganda. This student hated order, law, morality, and the family. He was an anarchist. He hoped to work for the eventual destruction of the American regime. Like many anarchists, his two main opponents were the family and religion. The Rhodes scholarship was a mechanism for acquiring power so that one day he could level society. He organized the political rally only to win the Rhodes scholarship to serve his future career as a political subversive.

The acronym for the march was the UGLU March, so we will call him the UGLU guy. When the UGLU guy walked into the neighborhood meetings, the old man would put his arm around the UGLU guy, help him out and give him things, even though the UGLU guy was doing what he could do to undermine this man's neighborhood, and was planning on getting a Rhodes scholarship so that he could implement policies that would destroy the old man's family, the neighborhood he lived in, and the religion he believed in. Also, from the point of view of his actual philosophical ideas, the UGLU guy was working against everything this man stood for. But this old man just thought, "Well he is a student of my University. I am a loyal alumnus of my University. So if he is a product of this University, I have to support him." Ironically, the adjunct was perceived by both for some reason as being the enemy.

The man's attitude was, "I have to mistreat my enemies and treat my friends well, even if my friend is a lion who will devour me someday."

It is a very barbaric approach to life.

With respect to *The Apology*, the old man represents the common citizen of Athens, the adjunct represents Socrates, and the UGLU guy is a Sophist. If we were to add the local journalists, TV studio, and a local playwright to the mix, we would have a fuller picture of the kind of people that united to put Socrates on trial. This triangle of relationships gets us closer to the dynamic of *The Apology*.

CHAPTER SIX

"UNTIL SOMEONE GIVES up drinking, stuffing oneself, sex and idleness, there will be no help in drugs, burning or cutting, pendants, or anything else of the sort." Plato, *Republic*, Book IV

"But take heed to yourselves lest your hearts be weighed down with dissipation and drunkenness and cares of this life, and that day come upon you suddenly like a snare. Luke 21:34

Alcoholism

Going back again to the *Protagoras*, Socrates says, "Relativism and deconstructionism is similar to going to a second rate drinking party where everybody is drinking just to get drunk. The music is so loud they cannot talk, and they just get drunk. A first rate drinking party would be one where the wine makes you just merry enough that you can have a good conversation and get to the truth of things."

If you are truly interested in growing in virtue, then one of your primary concerns should be to learn about your basic passions and emotions, and how to properly order them so that you can do what is true and good. One of the essential virtues is temperance, which teaches us how to properly order our passions and emotions with respect to food, drink, and marital reproduction. One of the passions most obviously out of control is the desire for alcoholic drinks. And so, it is worth discussing some aspects of the disorders associated with alcohol, perhaps as an example that could help us understand the disorders associated with our other basic passions.

If you are an alcoholic, you will find everything I have to say difficult and you will try to argue against it. If you are not an alcoholic, you still might not understand alcoholism, but it is worth it to get to know this disease. You are likely to know at least one alcoholic in your life, and knowing the disease can be helpful for knowing how to treat it. In addition, there is an analogy between the way that alcohol can take possession of the soul and the way that any passion, physical or spiritual, can take possession of the soul. There is, therefore, an analogy between how to overcome this disease and how to overcome any disease of the soul, be it physical, psychological or spiritual.

Most conservative estimates state that one in seven people is born with alcoholic dispositions. It is a disposition, a sickness or a disease that is misunderstood. But it is worth trying to address now the question of whether you have that disposition. In the ideal situation, if you were an alcoholic you would learn how to deal with it properly and you would actually deal with it properly. If you were not an alcoholic you would at least try to drink with some sense of responsibility.

Johns Hopkins University Hospital has developed a test for alcoholism. The test is available on the Internet. The results of the test are very simple. If the test taker answers "yes" to any of the questions, it is a definite warning of possible alcoholism. If the test taker answers "yes" to any two of the questions, the chances are likely that the test taker is an alcoholic. If a person answers "yes" to three or more questions, then it is almost definitely the case that he is an alcoholic.

If you are an alcoholic you will seize on the "almost." In fact, if someone answers "yes" to three or more questions that person is *definitely* an alcoholic. He should return to the home page and finish reading it, but also go to an Alcoholics Anonymous meeting immediately. If you are an alcoholic, the best programs for understanding the disease and getting over it are those administered in conjunction with Alcoholics Anonymous.

It is important to remember that alcoholism is a disease. The human person is composed of body and soul. We are not just physical bodies or spiritual souls. We can speak about any disease inasmuch as it has spiritual, psychological and physical dimensions. In this way, we can understand original sin to be a disease of the soul. Concupiscence, the disordered attraction to created things, is an effect of that disease. We all have original sin and concupiscence. Whether you like it or not, your nature is somehow attracted to do what is evil. Your nature is not evil but there is a disorderly inclination in it to do what is evil.

We also have bodies. That means you might have some physical dispositions over which you have no control. You may have one leg that is longer than the other. That is your disposition. You may not be a natural athlete; you are never going to play in the NFL or the NBA. You may have a predisposition to have a heart attack when you are 50 years old. If that is a physiogenetic disorder there is nothing you can do about it.

There are also some disorders that are partly physical and partly psychological, as well as partly spiritual. We are not simply material beings, or simply spiritual beings. We are encompassed in a body and spirit. It would make sense that we have or could have some dispositions that are a little physical and a little spiritual at the same time. For instance, if you are a manic depressive it is not because you have any say in the matter. That is how you are built. The only thing you can do is learn how to deal with it. If you are a diabetic all you can do is deal with it—eat properly, exercise enough, take insulin, and hope you do not go blind.

A friend of mine who understands genetics tells me that each person has on the average 60 genetic disorders. Alcoholism is one of these disorders. It is a disorder with physical and spiritual dimensions. I am sorry to say that if you have the disposition you have to learn how to deal with it, both physically and spiritually. To deal with alcoholism requires, more than anything, a spiritual program where you basically learn to rely on God.

Alcoholics Anonymous

Alcoholics Anonymous is the most effective way to deal with alcoholism. It is based on the spiritual: trust in God, realizing that this condition and its effects are beyond your control, putting everything in God's hands, making an examination of conscience, confessing your sins to somebody, and struggling to grow in virtue. The response is basically the spiritual life, but going through the struggle with others who are in similar circumstances, other alcoholics.

Alcoholism is a little like diabetes. There are some diabetics who are born with a disposition; for some people it manifests itself when they are nine, and for some others when they are 40 or 50. It can manifest itself at different times of a person's life. It is also true that there are some people who have such a poor diet that they effectively become diabetic. And they say that your generation will have a higher incidence of diabetes than previous generations because of all that high fructose corn syrup that is in practically everything that you eat and drink. So that is your fate—diabetes, alcoholism and blindness. You have that to look forward to.

Jokes aside, the same thing applies to alcohol: there are some people who might be able to drink themselves into alcoholism through their abusive behavior. How does this apply to us? If you have an alcoholic disposition the only way you can deal with it is to never drink again. Alcoholics are famous for rationalizing and for coming up with excuses. I know one alcoholic whose way to take this test is to think that if he can answer one or two questions properly, if he can change his behavior in one question then he is doing OK. So he says, "I never drink alone," because alcoholics drink alone. Alcoholics sleep in late after they drink, so he says, "I do not do that. I get up early in the morning. Even if I drink a lot I get up early in the morning. So those are two signs that I am not an alcoholic."

The problem with the one or two question approach is that it rationalizes away what is a serious issue. Again, studies on alcoholism indicate that most alcoholics are able to do one or two things very well for a long time, even if the rest of their lives are falling apart. Doing those one or two things well becomes the convenient rationalization for not treating the disease.

Set your own standards

From a moral standpoint you can almost argue that someone who is not an alcoholic and gets drunk is more morally responsible for his actions, is more culpable than alcoholic might be for his drunkenness. The non-alcoholic, the healthy person, knows what he is doing and does not have the cravings that alcoholics have; he does not have all the moral, physical, and physiological difficulties that an alcoholic might have.

If you know you are an alcoholic you should not drink anymore. You have to develop the means to not drink any more. The best way to do that is to become committed to a recovery program such as Alcoholics Anonymous, where you will work out with a sponsor what are the best activities for you to acquire so as to help you replace drinking alcohol.

If you are not an alcoholic, you should drink in moderation. You should limit yourself to one or two drinks. People asked Aquinas, "How many times in your life can a person really get drunk?" He said, "Probably one at the most. Once you are a mature man, between 18 and 22, the first time you get drunk you are doing it unintentionally. Then you know what your tolerance is and you can never purposely set out to get drunk again." This happens to most people at some point when they are out, perhaps at a party, having a good time. Aquinas was not against drinking, by the way. As a moral theologian he was all for partying and having a good time, in moderation.

A person's tolerance is going to be based a little on his physiological make-up. For most people, that probably means two to four drinks. I know some women who have gotten drunk on a glass of wine—that is their tolerance. But probably for most men I would guess it would be two to four drinks.

You have to set your own standards based on your physical disposition. Talk to someone who is prudent in these matters, such as a good priest, and then set your own limits. If you find yourself habitually drinking beyond your limit, then you have a problem.

It is also true that since the seventies, college culture has become a little bit worse with respect to drinking and drug abuse. This is in part because of the effect of *Animal House,* of which I spoke about earlier; and in part because of the drinking culture that is promoted; in part also because we have forgotten that there are many fine ways you can spend your leisure time outside of alcohol.

CHAPTER SEVEN

" L ET US THEN cast off the works of darkness and put on the armor of light; let us conduct ourselves becomingly as in the day, not in reveling and drunkenness, not in debauchery and licentiousness, not in quarreling and jealousy." Romans 13:12-13

Table Manners

In *The Republic* Socrates says, "We grow in virtue by getting up early in the morning." Bringing discipline to our daily routines assists our growth in fortitude, magnanaminity, wisdom.

It is not easy to spell out all the rules of table manners. There are no general principles. But, the whole point of table manners is to slow you down when you are eating, and to make eating a more social event. Manners eliminate a number of things that you are likely to do that are offensive or would lead to mistakes—that would make the place sloppier or make it uncomfortable for others. Ultimately, the whole point of the guidelines that make up table manners is to enable you to be more social, and to train you to start to think more about those around you than you think about yourself when you are eating.

For example, at the dorms when you go to the dining hall it is very rude to read when you are having dinner or lunch or breakfast while you are sitting with anyone. Many students develop the bad habit in college of reading the University newspaper instead of having a conversation with their friends. This is very impolite. You have very few social times. One of the great challenges of your college life, even though it could be hard at times, is to try to be more social, to learn how to have a conversation, and one of the times when you learn to have a conversation in a social setting is when you are at the table with someone.

By the way, the fruit of having good table manners is that if you use good table manners even in places like the dining hall, a well-bred, graceful girl will notice you, and she will notice how you eat even in the dining hall. There are definite marital benefits to having good table manners. You can quote me on that one.

In general, what I am going to suggest here are good table manners for America.

How I learned my table manners

My mother was attentive to table manners. She tried to teach them to me when I was a child and I partly heard her but mostly ignored what she taught me. When I was 19 I was just like you. I attended a class on virtue and leadership. I was fortunate to be around people who had good manners. They never talked about it but they ate with good manners so I probably by osmosis did just what they did. Their behavior re-inforced what I learned in the class.

When I was 20 or so I came home from college one break and was eating lunch or dinner with my mom. My mom asked me, "Where did you learn your good table manners?" I said, "What do you mean Mom? I don't know. You taught them to me . . . I don't know." She said, "Because your table manners are so much better than your brothers'. I mean, your brothers eat just like animals."

One of my brothers was probably 22 or so at the time and the other was 20. Although she never said anything to them, she noticed their lack of table manners. She just did not know what to say or she did not want to say anything. So I said, "Mom, I took one of these classes; and then I probably see good people who live these manners without ever talking about it; so by good example."

Then she asked me for my course outline and invited my two brothers over for dinner. Throughout the meal she taught them manners. And they made fun of her the whole way through the lesson, but they learned the basic guidelines for table manners.

Setting the table

There is a proper way to set the table.

The forks go on the left, and you pick up forks going from left to right towards your plate. If there is a salad fork, it will be to the left of the main fork. The dessert fork usually goes between the fork for the main course and the plate. On the right side of the plate, you get your spoons and knives. The knife is closest to the plate. Sometimes, the soup spoon and teaspoon are placed to the right of the knife. The wine glass and the water glass should be above the plate to the center. Sometimes the dessert utensils can go above the plate. This would be the simple table setting.

Here are some guidelines in no particular order. First, a big rule that men are bad at following: When setting a table, food should be served in dishes, bowls and pitchers, and not in the containers that they came in. Ideally, if you are setting a table, rather than just putting the gallon of milk out on the table you would actually put milk into a pitcher, or serve the orange juice into a pitcher and not the carton. If you have a package of cold cuts you would not just put it out in the plastic—you would put it out on a plate.

Now every home has its own unique customs. A small plate should be put under things like ketchup, mustard, or sauces. If it is a regular or family meal, you can put ketchup and mustard on a plate. My mom will always buy ketchup and mustard in a jar so that she can put them on a plate and then put them out.

Here are some rules on butter knives and sugar spoons. When you have breakfast and you want sugar for your tea and you ask somebody for sugar, or if somebody asks you for sugar, you just do not pass them the sugar. You also pass them the famous sugar spoon. You use the sugar spoon to put sugar in the tea or coffee and then put it down on the table. You then pick up your spoon and you stir with it. The same thing—having a knife for the serving dish—applies to butter, peanut butter, jelly and such.

Now ideally if you were ever girlfriend or significant other, when you are done with the main course you remove all the plates used during the main course. You take them to the kitchen, and then bring out the dessert plates.

Serving dinner

Ideally there is a main person at the table. It is usually the parent; at work it could be the director. You give the main dish to that person first. The person should take it and put the serving plate on his left and there will be two utensils, usually a big fork and a big spoon. You should use both of them: the spoon goes under the food and the fork goes on top of the food and you transfer it to the plate.

The idea is to hold the serving plate as close to the plate as possible. Usually, a serving plate with food on it will also have two utensils, a large fork and a large spoon, to accompany the plate. Use both utensils to put your food on the plate. Do not stab the food to put it on the plate. Instead, place the fork under the piece or pieces of food and the spoon on top. Do not slide the food from the serving plate to your plate. Instead, lift the food off the serving plate and place it on your plate.

If you violate these serving rules, nine times out of ten nothing happens. But the one time that it happens, it matters. Food slides off onto your plate or you get goop on the tablecloth. Avoid stabbing, sliding, or trying to balance food on the spoon. Normally, you pass the food to the person on your left. Everybody does not just go and grab food, or take something for himself and pass it around any old way. And then the serving goes around clockwise. The idea is to keep it moving.

The meat course

The proper way—in the U.S.—to cut when you have meat on your plate is to hold the fork with your left hand. Do not do it horizontally, or completely vertically either.

Put your knife on the top of your plate when you are done with it. Then, switch hands and put the meat in your mouth with your right hand. The point is to slow yourself down so that you speak with the others at the table. The European style is to take the meat with your left hand and go straight to your mouth.

Normally we eat chicken and spare ribs with a knife and a fork unless we're at a cookout or at a fast food restaurant. I guess the University dining hall is a kind of fast food restaurant. If any meat has a bone on it, it is acceptable to pick up the bone with your fingers to reach parts you cannot reach with your fork and knife. However, this should be kept to a minimum. Ideally, avoid this if you can.

If you are in a very formal setting and if you are really trying to impress a girl, and especially if you are at her house for the first time for dinner, do not pick up the bone. If you are at a formal event, do not order ribs. If you are served them at a formal event eat just a little bit and then go out to a barbeque rib shop afterwards.

Talking while eating

Do not talk with your mouth full. Try not to speak while you are chewing. And if someone asks you a question while there is food in your mouth you simply delay your reply until after you swallow.

A corollary of this rule is that you do not ask somebody a question as they are putting food into their mouth. It is impolite to do so.

Never "talk" with your fork and knife—put them down and chew.

Another important thing is that while there is food in your mouth, do not drink. It can be unattractive and dangerous to drink with food in your mouth. If your steak is tough, put sauce on it or ask for another steak. If you feel that you have to have something in your mouth, put a little bit of water in your mouth and then take a bite.

This might be a little mortification you have to live with while eating—there may just be a lot of tough stuff in your mouth. The reason not to drink when there is food in your mouth is that when you drink sometimes the food comes out and then your guests have to look at particles of food floating in your water. The other thing could be that your food could get stuck on the rim of the glass and that is a perfect way to turn a girl off.

You will start noticing these manners violations all over the place. You may notice that you yourself are doing some of these things.

Bread and butter

In Europe you can keep bread next to your plate on the tablecloth. In the U.S., generally you would keep it on a bread plate or on the side of your plate, and you would keep your serving of butter next to the bread.

There is usually a separate butter knife. Take the butter with the butter knife. Put the butter on your plate or on the bread plate and then pass the butter knife and the butter to the next person. Then, take your knife and you put the butter on the bread one bite at a time. We are not barbarians. We are not eating to be ready for bed or what is going to take place in 10 minutes. So the bread is broken into bite size pieces and each piece is buttered before being eaten.

If the bread is really hard, technically you are still supposed to break it and eat it.

There is one exception to this rule. If something is served hot, like toast, you can butter it all at once.

Dessert

The U.S. has deviated from its original refinement on the point of eating fruit for desesrt. For dessert if you order fruit, it is actually better to use a fork and knife to cut up your fruit and eat it rather than just chomping it. Even a banana—peel it and cut it up. If fruit is eaten on the run, it may be handled.

If cookies are served for dessert, wait till you get your dessert plate before you take your cookies. Put your cookies on your plate. You will see people who pick up cookies and put them on the table. This should not be done.

Corn on the cob

If you are served corn on the cob at a cookout, just eat it. Your hosts understand you are going to eat it with your hands. Usually at formal dinners they will serve corn with handles.

It is inappropriate to floss at the table.

Breakfast

At breakfast, if you are in a situation where you have a cereal bowl on a plate, it is better to finish the cereal before you start putting food on the plate.

Food on clothing

Should some food fall onto your clothing, if it can be carefully removed with a clean fork or spoon, that is the best way to remove it. If it is dry and you can pick it with your fingers that is all right.

If there is a danger of spotting, pull out your napkin, get it a little wet and try to blot it a little. But whatever you do, try not to turn it into a major laundry operation. Do not draw too much attention to yourself.

Smoking

Most people do not smoke during meals anymore. If you are in a place where they allow smoking, it is best not to smoke in between courses, unless there is a long gap in between courses.

Whether to smoke in between courses or during a course is a judgment call depending on the place where you are eating. Whatever the house rules are, follow them.

After dinner

Here is a big one: if you do not want coffee or tea, it is actually more appropriate, if they come by to serve it, to just put your hand there and say no, or "No thank you, please." But it is not appropriate to turn the cup over.

Now, there could be exceptions to this rule. For example, if the place is very crowded or if you are at a place like a banquet hall, it is better to just turn it over. But in general it is better to just say yes or no or indicate with your hands.

Napkin

If you have to cough or gag while eating, use your napkin to cover your mouth.

When eating ribs, any meat with sauce on it, or fried chicken it is not appropriate to lick your fingers. Use a napkin. At the end, use a wet napkin or go wash your hands. Fine restaurants will give you water and a little dipping bowl for your fingers.

If you are not going to reuse your napkin after the meal, just leave it next to your plate when you are done, not on the plate. I suggest that it be left in such a way that it is clear that it has been used but it should not be excessively disheveled.

Etc.

Small food: Small amounts of food that are hard to pick up with a fork like peas, kidney beans, and things like this can be pushed on to a fork with a piece of bread or with your knife. But do not use your fingers.

Removing food from mouth: If you happen to put something that cannot be chewed or is indigestible into your mouth it is best to remove it discreetly with whatever was used to put it in your mouth. So if you are eating chicken with your fingers you can use your fingers to discreetly take the bone out of your mouth. But if you can pull it off with a fork you will impress that millionaire girl who is very attractive.

Food you dislike: If you end up putting something in your mouth that you do not like because of the taste or it is too tough, you should still eat it. Do your best to chew on it and swallow it.

Another considerate guideline here is that you should make a reasonable effort to eat everything that you put on your plate.

Emptying a bowl: Do not scrape the ice cream bowl of every little drop of ice cream. Whenever you are emptying a bowl of anything, tip it away from you so that you do not spill things on your lap. When you tip it away from you it slows you down and you cannot just bury your face into your plate. Always avoid any motion that leads you to bury your head in your plate or bowl. Things like gravy, egg yolk, sauces—you cannot use your bread to mop those things up. Now if you want to be super-refined you would mop up your gravy by taking the bread and using your fork.

Ambiguous situations

The ultimate principle for knowing what to do in a situation in which you are not sure what to do: Look out of the corner of your eye and see what the hostess is doing, and then do that.

If you are in a dilemma as to what to do, just look at what other people are doing and do what they are doing. At the same time, if you know that what they are doing is vulgar or it is not appropriate, do not do the opposite—do whatever whoever has the authority is doing in that situation.

By the way, you will probably find that there are many people who do not do these little things. However, when you are sitting with polite company it is better to act this way. And if there is some girl you want to impress when you are doing this, she will notice, I promise you.

The real test

The real test would be this. Go home and eat with good manners in front of your mother without saying anything, and see if she notices. OK, now when I took this test when I was 19, for the next two weeks when we ate together we spent most of our meals correcting each other. If done in a fun-filled way, this could be a way to train each other for more serious situations. So, try to live these guidelines with your friends in the dining halls. Talk about them with people. It will be a simple way to start conversations with people, and it will help you practice so that you can show your good manners in situations that matter.

CHAPTER EIGHT

" **B**UT THE FRUIT of the Spirit is love, joy, peace, patience, kindness, goodness, faithfulness, gentleness, self-control; against such there is no law. And those who belong to Christ Jesus have crucified the flesh with its passions and desires." Galatians 5: 22-24

Friendship

Recall St. Josemaria's words that "laymen have to first learn how to pray, they have to develop contemplative souls." If they do not have souls of prayer, rather than transforming society according to the order that is in their souls, they will either get sucked up by that society and adopt its unchristian customs, or they will so compromise their faith that they will simply project the disorder that is in their souls onto society. Friendship involves friendship with God—learning how to pray—and building order in the soul through our relationships with others.

A lot of college graduates look back and say, "Oh! I loved my four years at college. I made so many friends." If you asked such a person, "Who are your friends?," they will not have any answers.

It is not that they do not have friends. They have friends, but their idea of the meaning of friendship is distorted. They lack the proper friendship with God. Therefore, they do not see how they can become friends with those around them. They fail to see the way in which their friendships participate in their friendship with God. I really think this is true. You will read about this in the *Symposium* (especially 199-223). These pages correspond to the final two interventions of the dialogue, the intervention of Socrates, in which he relays to the others a conversation he once had with Diotima, and then, the interruption by Alcibiades, in which Alcibiades insults and praises Socrates at the same time.

Socrates claims that he had a conversation once with an old Athenian lady, Diotima. She teaches Socrates in the *Symposium* that the highest kind of love, and therefore the highest kind of friendship, is a friendship that has the noblest things in the soul in common. The kind of children that such a friendship produces is one based on noble ideas. The children that such a friendship produces are the virtues that grow in the soul of each person. The soul is spiritual. The highest thing in it is the virtues. Therefore, a friendship that is truly a friendship will be one in which each person inspires, cajoles, encourages, and helps the other to grow in virtue. In the best friendships, both friends are doing this for each other.

The Ideal Friend

One notion that emerges from the *Symposium* is that there is an ideal friend. Every other kind of friendship is a participation in this ideal just as there is an ideal love. And every other kind of love is a participation in this ideal.

In my opinion, Christ is the ideal friend. At the Last Supper, he teaches the Apostles what it means to be a friend—a friend is a servant. He even says to his disciples, "I do not call you servants, I call you my friends." He proceeds to serve them by washing their feet. He also tells them, "No greater love does a man have than he lay down his life for his friends."

I would like to propose a model of friendship between males: The best kind of friendship you can be involved in with another man is a kind of brotherly love, in the true sense of the word "brother," in which each is trying to help the other's soul give birth to virtue. You are like a midwife, or a brother who is helping the other learn and live virtue.

This is what Christ was doing for his Apostles, how he was serving them. This is how you would have to not just conceive of yourself, but truly be towards those around you. This is difficult to do.

Types of Friendship

In his *Nicomachean Ethics*, Aristotle makes the basic distinction that there are three kinds of friendship—those based on pleasure, those based on utility, and those based on virtue.

Friendships based on pleasure are those where there could be physical pleasure between two people. For instance, friends do pleasurable things together, such as drinking together.

Friendships of utility are those where each person is using the relationship, often for economic gain. My father was a bar owner. He once told me of a man named Roger who was the Liquor Control Commissioner of the State of Michigan. My dad remarked that it was amazing that when Roger was the Commissioner, everybody was his friend. Thousands of people showed up at his retirement party. But at his funeral there were few people. So a lot of Roger's friends were friends of utility. They were his friends because he was the Liquor Control Commissioner, and they were bar owners. They wanted to make sure their bar licenses were in order. They probably came to his retirement party to make sure that they would meet his successor. You will see this throughout life. There are a lot of people who become friends because of business relationships or because of mutual interest so that they can make money or something similar.

In college, you probably will see more of the pleasure-based relationships. Aristotle says in the *Nicomachean Ethics* that young people are, more often than not, in pleasure-based friendships. The passions are stronger in young people, and they can subconsciously imagine that the people around them who please their passions are their friends. A sign of this is that they just spend a lot of time with each other because it is pleasurable. They do things together that they like.

There is nothing wrong with the first two kinds of friendship. But in the end these are just participations or reflections of what true friendship is—friendship based on virtue. This idea, as well as this practice, is becoming less and less apparent as part of what would be considered custom in America.

Friendships of virtue

One sign that friendship is falling out of our customs and culture is that we are losing sight of the reality of virtue, especially in our institutions and our educational system. Virtue is an idea, a concept that we use to describe something that is true, habits or dispositions to do what is good.

You can have virtues and may not realize it. The difference between knowing what virtue is, and cultivating it, versus not knowing what it is and leaving its occurrence to chance, is the difference between an apple tree growing in the wild to a similar tree growing in the orchard of an apple company.

When I was growing up my Dad bought an apple orchard from an apple company. The company was in its last year of cultivating the trees. There were beehives around the orchard because bees help pollinate the apple blossoms, so that each tree can produce many apples. There were safeguards to keep animals away from the trees and harmful insects off the trees. The orchard was constantly making sure that the apple trees would produce fruit. One year later, the orchard was left to grow wild. The beehives disappeared. Weeds grew beneath the trees. Many of them died. Some trees produced fruit, but many of the apples had worms in them. They were, essentially, wild trees. The trees growing in the wild may have borne fruit, but they were more susceptible to blight. Their fruit were smaller. The trees growing in the orchard when it was being cultivated were better cared for. They bore more and better fruit.

Likewise, a society that loses the notion of virtue is going to become like the tree growing in the wild. There may be fruit but it is going to be much more haphazard than a society where there are customs that encourage virtues.

Friendships of Fondness

There is one kind of friendship that you want to be most wary of—the friendship of fondness. That is the friendship between a man and a woman from a young age, which St. Francis de Sales says is a kind of friendship that prevents both souls from maturing and the ultimate end of which is sin, even if it could take five to ten years. But this is one of the bigger dangers of the modern friendship scene.

The "friendship of fondness" is basically a quasi-relationship, a friendship between a man and a woman, or a young man and a young girl, where they show affection for each other—it does not have to be physical affection—that is really beyond what might be a basic relationship between a young man and a young woman.

Its purpose is not really courtship with a view to marriage. It is just a friendship. Sometimes it is exclusive—the only person you hang out with is a person of the opposite sex. I know two people who have been involved in such a relationship for 21 years. There is no marriage or engagement but they do not really spend time with anybody else either. So, I am not saying that we should not have acquaintances with women. I am saying that before entering into a friendship with a young lady, you should think about whether you are ready to see this friendship lead to marriage. Part of this equation also consists of having some confidence that it is your vocation to marry. Otherwise, you should be aware that you are entering into a friendship that poses difficulties for the maturation of your own soul as well as your capacity to make friends with other males.

Best friends

There usually are a few people in our lives who over time we call our best friends. If these are healthy friendships and do not lead to clique behavior, it is all right. In some sense, if we have a good friendship with one person, our goal should be to make more friends with whom we have a deep friendship like that person. Not that we neglect that person; however, we should seek to have more friends than the one or two we might currently have. We should do this because the human heart is capable of expansion. If we are growing in virtue, we should be able to make friends with other men.

Christ had twelve Apostles whom he called his friends. Obviously, he sought more and he could make us his friends too but he was closer to these twelve people; and even within the twelve it seems that there were some he had more affection for than the others; John, the beloved Apostle, James and Peter, for example. He let them in on things he did not let even the other Apostles in on.

The Notion of Friendship in Academia

Consider how friendship is studied in academia. Although Aristotle mentions friendship in his *Nicomachean Ethics*, it is a rarely mentioned topic in books on ethics during the last century. A friend of mine who wrote a book on ethics, politics and friendship had his graduate students examine the top one hundred books in ethics and philosophy in the 20th century. They examined the table of contents for chapters on friendship, but there were none. They then examined the indices of these books (in case the content on friendship was hidden behind fancy chapter titles), and only three books had two or three pages on friendship.

A professor at the University of Notre Dame considers friendship to be a very important part of his own study of philosophy. He has noticed that in philosophy conferences, the panels on friendship always have the same three people—in every panel, every year, in different conferences. This is important because, over time, the ideas of intellectuals tend to infiltrate or seep down into institutions, into practices, into laws, into popular education and into customs. However, intellectuals who are interested in friendship and ethics have decreased over the last two or three centuries.

In your own education, in the University, you may not find many classes or examples in classes about the ideal of friendship. For Plato, Aristotle, Aquinas or Augustine this would be problematic. Because the whole purpose of education is to prepare young women and men for friendship. Education ultimately should be both a moral and an intellectual preparation, so that you can be friends with the people you work with, with your fellow citizens and the political society, the Church that you belong to, and God. Therefore, if friendship is lacking, or training in friendship is lacking, your group or society at some point is going to be faced with a lot of problems.

Friendship and University life

It is important for males to develop friendships with males. A more and more frequent trend that I am noticing is that men are having a difficult time befriending other men. When I ask a lot of men who their best friend is, they usually mention a girl. Or if I ask them, "Who are you trying to help grow in virtue?" they will list girls.

There is a danger to that. If you really want to develop the virtues that make you a man, you need to become friends with other men.

Girls are a little more advanced than men as far as social capacity is concerned. This is a sociological reality. Girls are very good at relationships. In a book called *Brain Sex*, a feminist English reporter reports discovering studies that show that three-month-old female fetuses have chemicals running through their brains that set them to think of life in terms of relationships. In contrast, two-month-old male fetuses have chemicals running through them that condition them to think about conquering and protecting territory.

The point of this is that when a male grows up in a culture like ours, where the ultimate standard for evaluating action is feelings, he is ill-equipped to handle it. Whereas girls, from the time they are toddlers, are masters of feelings, of emotions. They are masters of learning how to make you feel good, of learning how to make you feel understood. It is therefore hard, at least when you are young, to establish a friendship with a girl based on equally challenging each other to grow in virtue.

There is nothing wrong with the fact in itself that girls can provide for certain emotional needs, but you need the friendship of another man. You need to become friends with someone who challenges you. Girls challenge you to learn how to love them, but they are not going to challenge you to be virtuous, at least at first. Once you are married they will, but then you will probably be running away from them. This is a problem of courtship and marriage, which we will entertain at another point. The importance of trying to establish friendship with other men partly lies in the fact that it is a sign that you are becoming self-motivated in virtue.

How is this discussion of friendship and virtue relevant to your life in the University? First, you must learn how to develop friends who are male. Second, you must learn to live a schedule. The reason to live a scheduled life is that you want to create time. You want to get your homework done so that you can create time to foster friendships and learn how to pray. You must start to be a little bit orderly in your life, not for the sake of being orderly, but so that you can actually start doing what is required to be friends with people.

Questions and Answers

Here are some questions my students have asked me about friendship, and my replies to them:

Q: How do you become friends with other men who do not have the same moral standards that you do? In our dorm, we hang out by sections. The guys in my section are big guys who drink a lot. I would not say that is a bad thing, but that is not who I am.

A: It is hard. You are not going to be friends with your dorm-mates based on virtue. All I can give are some practical guidelines. I cannot give definitive answers here but one thing I would say, with some people who you realize are not going to grow in virtue, but with whom you still want to establish a friendship, at some level you just have to do little favors for them to let them know that you are interested in them.

Whenever they want to start living virtue you will be there. It could be something as simple as sending them a postcard when you are home for the winter break. At this point, if they are just into the habits of drinking and things like that, they are not ready. But somehow they need to know that you are their friend; that you are waiting for them in case they ever want a break.

Second, I would say to become a friend with someone, you have to work at it. You have to say to somebody, "Let us meet for lunch," or "Let us go out for pizza or coffee." Then, within the context of these meals or meetings, which are like the good parties Socrates spoke of, you can try to start a conversation that would establish your friendship on a deeper level. Such a friend may be someone outside of your section.

When students want to live off campus, they often have the following dilemma: "All my friends are undergraduates who live in the dorm. If I live off campus, I will not be their friend anymore." I always say the same thing to these students. When you live off campus, you will discover who your real friends are. You will also discover the "work" involved in establishing and keeping real friends. Students, then, move off campus and they realize the truth of what I told them. Guys that stay at the dorm eventually realize the same thing. That in some sense the guys that are next to you, you want to become their friends, and you do not want to avoid them. But that is a little bit of a friendship of convenience.

So the friendships that you develop will be ones you make by saying, "Let us go have lunch together. Let us have dinner together." Or the ones where you say, "Let us go somewhere this weekend and study to get ready for our exams." Or you may want to play sports together or do your service project together, things like this. The real friends that you will develop are friends like that.

It could be as simple as, "This Friday night let us go smoke cigars and drink wine." Those are the two best activities in the world. You may ask, "Doesn't smoking kill?" But cigars do not kill.

Each kind of tobacco consumption conforms to a different part of the soul. Let me explain. The reality is that cigarette smoking conforms to the passions, whereas cigar smoking confirms to the will. Pipe smoking conforms to the intellect.

The kind of people who smoke cigars are usually the big guys. They like to be aggressive. Or you smoke a cigar to celebrate a victory or celebrate the birth of a child. That is an example of the will exerting itself. So cigars conform to the will.

A typical pipe smoker can be a professor who sits and reads while smoking his pipe—that is the intellect. I myself have a bunch of pipes in my office.

So pipe smoking conforms to the intellect and cigar smoking to the will, whereas cigarette smoking and tobacco chewing conform to the passions.

There was a study that was suppressed—an independent study about tobacco. The study discovered that cigarette smoking would make you live less than the average, cigar smoking the same as the average and pipe smokers live longer than the average.

Of course, a smart aleck may ask, "What if someone did all three?" In that case, I would propose that there be a new study. Maybe that would even it out. Maybe you should just smoke cigarettes and pipes.

The point of this digression is not simply to make a joke about tobacco. It is to illuminate a point that friends challenge each other to develop what is highest in each other. And so, true friends will help each other grow in virtue, which involves developing the intellect and the will. A great sign of the intellect is speech. And so, if smoking helps two friends to have a conversation, and thus exercise their intellects, then it is a potentially ennobling activity. What we need to do is to find the people who can really help us grow in virtue.

Going back to friendship, what I have discovered over the years is that with students who live off-campus or undergraduates who are in the dorms, the friends they develop are not necessarily the guys that simply live closest to them in the dorms. They could be but it is not necessarily the case. Usually the friends they develop are guys that they meet who basically have a common interest based on a class that they are in, or a group that they are in. And the friendship grows based on that common interest.

They are usually guys who are actively seeking more friends, so they do not limit themselves to just a small group of people who share one little common interest. Oftentimes they might have friends all over campus, or from different sections in the dorm, who might be doing different things. Because they are in class together, or they have had lunch together, it has developed into a friendship. They may have gone on a service project together with some other people, where they met somebody and they talked.

There are many different ways people from different parts of campus or from different groups can become friends with each other. But the one thing that is common to guys who become friends is that they are actively seeking them.

Suffering together also builds friendship. I have noticed from my classes over the years that friendships develop in my class because people suffer together!

Friendship often begins on the more basic level of utility. If you are helping each other—and some are better than others—eventually from there the friendship will grow. If two people are dedicated to living virtue and struggling to grow in virtue then they will not be equal. One guy will have more fortitude but the other guy will have more prudence. And so in that sense, just by their example, they will be challenging each other. So in a way there is never a strict equality between friends. The equality would be that the two are struggling to grow in virtue.

Q: What if in a friendship one friend has to put in more effort than the other?

That can happen too, but at the same time the friendship as a friendship will not advance, unless the two are putting the same effort into it. So if one puts more effort into it than the other, the one that is putting more effort into it has to wait for the other to start to reciprocate, because if you do not then you could start to become pushy. Thomas More at several points in his life realized this. We have letters that he wrote to "delinquent friends" in which he very politely explained to them that they needed to start seriously living virtue again, or their friendship could not advance. He basically said he was ready to walk arm in arm with them to help them live virtue, but that they had to make the commitment to do so for the friendship to advance.

CHAPTER NINE

" **B** RETHREN, DO NOT be children in your thinking; be babes in evil, but in thinking be mature." I Corinthians 14:20

Relationships

In this chapter, I discuss relationships with women, including marriage. I will also lay out some guidelines that you may follow in your relationships. For this, we look not to Plato's symbolic *Republic* as a guide, but to the *Symposium* (*A Plato Reader*, edited by Ronald B. Levinson, 1967, 112-154).

The Only Real Friendship?

Reading the *Symposium* would be a good basis for discussing the whole concept of dating and marriage. But we can also start with contemporary evidence. On November 7, 2006, the *New York Times* printed an Op-Ed on marriage entitled "Too Close For Comfort." In this piece, Stephanie Coontz claims that in the last hundred years or so there has been a real rise in the idea of marriage being the only real friendship in one's life. The author calls this the romantic notion of marriage. She suggests that this might be one important reason for the rise in divorce rates. Men and women expect that all their friendship should come from the same place, and when it does not happen, they look for a new romantic friendship that will satisfy them.

I do not think Stephanie Coontz is what we might call a conservative traditionalist. The author is a lady who is trying to look at the history of marriage. She notices that in the "bad old days," in addition to being married, people had a lot of friends among coworkers, extended family members, neighbors and acquaintances.

As there has been a rise in this "ideal" that the only place for real friendship or affection between a man and a woman is in the marital relationship, other kinds of friendships have broken down. Over time, the marriage also breaks down, because it does not provide for all of the needs of friendship that the person harbors.

In her final point, the author says that it was under the influence of Freudianism that a lot of people began to feel that only through marriage can all your instincts be fully satisfied. So people began to reject the claims of friendship of coworkers or family members, or people from the neighborhood or friends.

I do not agree with everything that the author has written, but in general her historical analysis is valid. It fits with what I am trying to communicate here, which is that we need friends outside of friendship with a female. We should look for friendships with other men and try to foster and help these friendships to grow. This is something that will help us mature.

The True Model of Manliness

I would also like to articulate something that is implicit in almost everything I am doing in this book. That "something" is the model of manliness or maturity that I am striving to articulate.

It is one thing to want to mature. It is another thing to discover and then to have an image in one's head about what maturity is. It is quite another thing to consciously take the steps to mold oneself into that image. The model I propose is the way of life of the first Christians. That is the true model of manliness or maturity that we should look to if we want to discover how to change our University or our society. They did change things and they did it right. If we are concerned at all about changing things we should look to them.

To give an example, in the opening chapters of the *Summa Contra Gentiles*, St. Thomas Aquinas reminds us that the ideal that we have for transforming ourselves and society is that of the first Christians. They truly lived and followed Christ. They lived His way of life, and "conquered" or won over the Roman Empire by peaceful means.

JEFFREY J. LANGAN

The first Christians are the model of true cultural change. They are the model of the standards of friendships that we should be striving for. They are the model of the standards by which we should try to be living our lives.

My model—the first Christians—does not use Catholicism as a mask for acquiring pleasure or for spreading Marxism or capitalism or becoming successful, or living a two-faced Catholicism—"I am Catholic on Sunday, work like a dog during the week, and then am a pagan on the weekends."

I remember when I was in college there were several books that we were told "we do not read anymore," and that we should not read them. Among the titles that we should not read any more were Pascal's *Pensees*, Plato's *Republic*, the books of Hillaire Belloc and Christopher Dawson, Jacques Maritain's *Three Reformers,* and St. Alphosus Ligouri's *Victory of the Martyrs*. Hearing this, I made it my mission to read these forbidden books. *So* of course I read them. So, those are books you should "not read." Please do "not read" *Victory of the Martyrs* by St.Alphonsus de Ligouri.

One of the interesting things about the book is that you get little vignettes. Sometimes the stories are two pages long and sometimes five. You will find these little stories of how the martyrs in Rome lived and died, and also the martyrs in Japan. In these little stories you get to see what they were willing to do or not do in order to show their love for Christ. And you can get a picture in your mind of their fortitude and their intelligence.

This is also why we are always encouraged to read and know the writings of the Fathers of the Church.

Read the Fathers of the Church

Many Christians in the United States, sad to say, are more familiar with the teachings of the American Founders than they are with the teachings of the Fathers of the Church. This is unfortunate because they fail to realize that many of the American Founders knew of and were deeply suspicious or even hated the teaching of the Fathers of the Christian Churches. Some of American Founders hoped that there new teachings would create a society and culture that replaced or forever negated the relevance of the teaching of the Fathers of the Church and the Christian Civilization that they helped found.

And yet, a Christian in the 21st Century or any well-meaning person could benefit greatly from reading and meditating on the writings of the Fathers of the Church. One such example deals with social and economic life.

People these days talk about the social doctrine of the Church. How did the Church develop its social doctrine? What did it do? A group of cardinals, bishops and theologians in the 19th century revisited the works of the Fathers of the Church, looking specifically at questions such as: *How did the Fathers of the Church teach Christians to act in political and economic ways? How did they teach the first Christians to act and work in society so as to show that they were Christian?*

While doing so, the 19th century cardinals, bishops and theologians read works such as the *Homilies* of St. John Chrysostom on the book of Matthew. Therein, he says to the Christians in Antioch something to the effect of: "You Christians are a bunch of fools. You are leaving the city and fleeing to the exterior. You leave your houses in the city, flee to the exterior and compete with one another over who can buy the biggest lots, and who can build the biggest houses. Then you compete with one another over who has the finely gilded golden chariots." Replace chariots with cars and you have yourself a very contemporary sounding teaching.

There is another passage in the same work in which Chrysostom says, "Do you know how bad things are getting for you men in the city of Antioch? Do you know what is happening these days? You are sending merchants out to Asia to buy lace at cheap prices—lace that is made by slaves. The merchants bring the lace from Asia and you buy the lace and put it on your shoes. You start competing with one another about who has the most nicely decorated lace shoes. Furthermore, a sign of the turpitude or the lowness to which we have gone is that we think that every man, even every poor man in the city has a right to have these finely laced sandals and shoes. If you men think that the kinds of shoes that you have are so important, maybe we should hang them from your ears and wear them as earrings like the women."

If we were to take these statements by Chrysostom, we could easily adapt them to modern social and economic conditions. In the United States, following the political and economic ideals espoused by the Founding Fathers, Christians compete with one another over who can move fastest to the suburbs, buy the biggest plots of land, and build the biggest home. In the modern global economy, we set up more sophisticated trade routes, making cheap shoes in China, Vietnam, or Guatamala. Rather than putting lace on our shoes, we change the styles every year. And finally, one of the great treasures of our poor or inner city youths is the regular competition over expensive and fashion designed basketball shoes. Chrysostom and the Church Fathers had a response to this problem. So did the Christians of the 19th Century, who, reflecting on the teachings of the Church Fathers came up with principles for guiding social and economic life. This became known as the Social Doctrine of the Church. And so, if you are concerned about justice in the areas of politics, economics, culture, and society, you would do well to reflect on the teachings of the Fathers of the Church, (to know their teachings at least as well as you know the teachings of the American Founders), as well as the principles of Catholic Social Teaching. This would give you excellent criteria for the political, cultural, economic, and social transformation of the society in which we live.

Read real philosophers

It is also revealing to read philosophers like Plato and Aristotle. Earlier I suggested that it is extremely important to study the Classics. But it is important for you to know that beginning in the 20th century the teaching of Classics in this country, along with much of the educational establishment, was by and large taken over by followers of Rousseau, Nietzsche, and Dewey and they did everything they could do to use education in general and the study of the Classics in particular to promote an understanding of the human person that is counter to the Platonic, Aristotelian, and Christian understanding of the human person.

Plato, Aristotle and Cicero were no longer taught in Classics departments because the philosophy of these thinkers was too close to Catholicism. I have a friend who teaches the history of education in America and Europe here at the University. He has written articles and books on the kind of war that went on in the late 19th and early 20th century to get Plato and Aristotle expelled from the Classics departments.

When I was living in New York City in the early 1990s, feminists started quoting from *The Bacchae*. *The Bacchae* is the mantra of feminism in our times. It tells the story of women who run off to the hills in order to participate in Dionysian revelry. Of course, in doing so, they end up tearing the males who come after them limb from limb. Perhaps the most dramatic part of the play is when one of the women, Agave, returns to her senses only to find the head of her son in her lap. In her bacchic frenzy, she had torn it off. This, I think, is a fitting image of where feminism can lead us.

Thomas Carlyle was a vehement anti-Catholic who wrote a history of England and ended up being the administrator of India in the late 19th century. He lost his faith at one point and became a follower of Nietzsche. When Carlyle went to India, his sister died and he read Euripides to console himself—he read and re-read and meditated on the plays of Euripides for five years. At one point, he was put in charge of writing the laws for India. He then tried to write Euripidean laws for the colony of India—he tried to liberalize divorce, make homosexuality legal, not penalize adultery, allow for contraception, and loosen up economic relations so that it was easier to grind the poor. He implemented the "divide and conquer" mentality in India.

Ironically, in order for his laws to be promulgated in India, his friends back in England had to actually liberalize the English laws, because in the English legal system the laws in a colony cannot be more liberal than the laws in the mother country. It is these laws that Carlyle had promulgated in India and the ones that followed in its footsteps were the ones that Gandhi was protesting against: these modern-secularist human laws that were abandoning Platonic and Aristotelian notions of justice and friendship and were implementing a more pre-Socratic vision of the world.

The Symposium

The *Symposium* is a Platonic dialogue in which Plato critiques several limited notions of love. It gives us an excellent insight into the true notion of love. The dialogue consists of a series of speeches about love. The various speakers pronounce their views of the ideals of love, using medicine to intensify the experience of love, the erotic nature of love, as well as the origins of the desire we have within us that leads us to seek a "soul mate." Then, Socrates intervenes, hinting that most of the speakers have not spoken accurately about love because they failed to define it and because they failed to understand its spiritual rather than physical dimension. The implication is that each of the speakers either possesses a character defect, an intellectual defect, or both, and these lead them into a flawed notion about love.

JEFFREY J. LANGAN

How to read Platonic dialogues

As an aside, this is a key to reading all the dialogues of Plato. In almost every conversation Socrates meets a person who has a character defect, an intellectual defect or both that prevents that person from seeing the truth of the matter. If you, the reader, can figure out what that defect is, you can better understand why the dialogue ends in apparent failure as well as what defect you, the reader, should avoid if you ever hope to arrive at the truth of the matter that Socrates and the other characters in the dialogue discuss. There is almost always an implicit critique of the characters in the dialogue and the sophistical positions that they represent. If you can keep this in mind, you can read the dialogues of Plato with great profit.

That is where most Cabbalistic or modern readers of Plato's dialogues go wrong. They basically say that there is an implicit critique of Christianity in the Platonic dialogues, which is absurd because Christianity was not around at that time. Or, they read the dialogues as if Plato put in them a secret teaching subversive of a just social order. You will be a much more sensitive reader of the dialogues if you read the dialogues as an implicit critique of Sophistry because the Sophists actually were living at that time. It is pretty clear in the dialogues that those are the enemies we have to deal with here.

With this hint in mind, and after a long aside, we can now discuss the *Symposium*.

The Speeches in the Symposium

There are five speeches in the *Symposium*.

The *Symposium* is set at the house of Agathon. Agathon had just won the prize for "Best Tragedian" in 416 B.C. A group of Athenian men come to his house. These men are, by and large, students of the Sophists of Athens. We know from the dialogues that some of them are homosexual lovers. Someone proposes that they give speeches on love.

Most of the speeches in the *Symposium*, except for the speech of Socrates, are speeches that are basically sophistical, meaning there is some aspect of the speech that is wrong, but the Sophists are trying to promote it as something normal.

The first speech basically says love is a fulfillment of desire and instinct, and the reason that customs are good is because customs slow down desire and instinct. The first speech is the "man-boy love association" speech. The highest form of love is the man-boy love association, because it is the kind of love that enables one to basically get pure pleasure with no consequences. No baby can be born in the man-boy love association. What the man-boy love association is looking at is the fulfillment of instincts. What the first speech argues is that there should be customs that are put in place that recognize this love relationship, i.e. same-sex marriage, so that it slows down the way one gives into instincts.

The next speech is what I call the "Viagra speech." The Bob Dole of Athens says that love is a chemical concept and we should use medicines to replenish the body so that a guy can get attracted if and when he wants to, and his attractions never run out.

Then we get the speech of Aristophanes, which says that you are built the way you are by genetics; that there are two kinds of human nature. We were all born Tasmanian devils and have now become the way we are. He says that originally there were three kinds of humans. Every human was a sphere and everybody had double what they have right now—four eyeballs, two noses, two mouths, four legs and four arms. Your head and your middle section were spheres. People got around by spinning around like the Tasmanian devil in the Bugs Bunny cartoon.

In one group of people the two sides were both male, and in another group one side was male and one side female. In the third group, both sides were female. Because of their pride, Zeus decided to cut everybody in half. He then turned their heads around, turned their mid-sections around, and then the belly button and the chest; that is where he sewed everybody up so they would be whole again.

According to this tale, lesbians were all the people who came from the two-sided females. Male homosexuals were all those who came from the two-sided males. Heterosexuals were the ones who came from the two-sided beings that had a different sex on each side.

Aristophanes says that everybody now is seeking their other half. Sometimes you get this pagan notion, "Oh, he is the one," or "Oh, she is the one." Or, "I am looking for or have found my soul mate." Aristophanes' tale is where we get this notion that everybody is seeking their other half—they are seeking the one that will make them whole.

What is interesting about this speech of Aristophanes is that he recognizes that love implies unity or wholeness. Towards the end of his speech he says people are not ultimately seeking sexual pleasure. What they are seeking is a kind of wholeness and this wholeness or unity does not come from sex. It comes from something else. But ultimately what people are seeking is unity; they are seeking wholeness again. They want to become Tasmanian devils again like in the good old days.

Then Agathon speaks. Agathon is a classic Sophist—he just says a lot about love he does not believe. But a lot of it sounds pretty good. "Someone who loves should be refined, they should be graceful. They should live the virtues—temperance, prudence, fortitude, justice. Someone who loves will become young again even if he is very old."

Then everybody turns to Socrates. They say, "Socrates, what do you think about all this?"

What Love Is

In almost every Platonic dialogue involving Socrates, there is an implicit critique of the other speeches. He brings out what is true in all the others' speeches. He puts it all together and he gives you all the pieces. If you can think and put them together you will understand the true teaching.

Socrates says that all the previous speeches do not speak about what love is. They just speak about the qualities of love; they just give rhetorical praise to love. Socrates says he is going to explore what love is:

Love is when one has a desire for an object that one currently does not possess. That is what love is. I have a desire for something that I currently do not possess. I expect that some day I can possess that good. This could be something that is right now or it could be something in the future. But if I love someone right now, I expect that in the future I will also have their love. Love is not just of beautiful things, it is of *good* things. Love is also of truth, of beauty, of good and of wholeness.

Notice that the four transcendentals are implied in love: truth, beauty, goodness, and unity.

You may say that Socrates describes lust. But lust is a disorder desire that arises for pleasure. Love is just a desire I have for the good. It is love in a very simple, experiential sense of the word.

Love based on passion

In the *Phaedrus* (the dialogue that follows the *Symposium* in the order of the dialogues), Socrates gives this great description of love that is based on passion. He describes it as between a man and a boy, and he eventually critiques this notion of love. If you replace the word "boy" with the word "girl," and you just take man and woman, especially college students, he describes almost perfectly the typical type of abusive relationship that you see among guys and girls in college. The guy becomes dominating, he makes the girl his slave, he gets angry at her all the time, he makes her do disgusting things, he makes her promises that he will never keep, they both become obsessed with each other, they basically make each other lose their attachment to friends and family so that they are always spending time with each other all day long. Socrates really nails it.

This is a kind of romantic relationship which we all should be careful of, as the author describes in the editorial of the *New York Times*.

Socrates and Diotima

Keeping in mind the speeches from the *Symposium*, Socrates' definition of love, and the abusive relationship described in the *Phaedrus*, we can now understand Diotima's explanation of love.

Socrates says that when he was a younger man he met Diotima. Diotima was an old lady who was a prophet. She figured out how to keep Athens free from the plague for ten years—the implication here is that if you love in the wrong way you will be hit by a kind of plague. I think from a medical standpoint you would say it is syphilis. But the implication here is also that there is a spiritual plague that can beset your soul if you love in the wrong way.

Unitive Love

Diotima says that true love is really happiness. True love is when a person possesses what is true: truly true, truly good and truly beautiful. She says that love is first of all a spiritual thing. It is neither godly nor human, but a spiritual thing. This is because the highest thing in a man is his soul; and the soul is a spiritual being, a spiritual entity. So whatever makes the soul happy is what the soul desires. The soul desires what is like it. If the soul is spiritual, then what it desires, the good that it expects, should be spiritual as well.

Diotima goes on to say that love is a way of poverty, because the soul always desires things and in some sense its desire is never really satisfied. It is always seeking an object which it does not get. Diotima says, "The example of a lover is a philosopher who in his best moments loves the truth, and is searching for it. He somewhat gets it but he never fully gets it. He partly knows the truth and is partly ignorant of it, but he keeps pursuing his love."

Diotima says to Socrates, "The ultimate kind of love is love for *logos*—reason, truth, beauty, order. It is the reason that governs the Universe. Ultimately, true love would be the spiritual love for *logos*. Desiring the highest kind of love is the desire to possess a spiritual good."

"The ultimate desire that the soul is seeking for is the desire to possess the good things and to be happy by possessing the good things." Diotima suggests that we all have this desire in our souls, but the problem is that we have to somehow train our soul so that we can let this desire for the good things lead us, so that this desire can reach its spiritual end. We tend to easily misinterpret this desire as a desire that will be fulfilled by material things or other creatures.

Diotima says what we are seeking is the love that would make the soul complete. This is unitive love. Playing off Aristophanes, she says that this is the love that will make us whole.

The love that leads us to the spiritual good is the one that will truly satisfy our soul. Any other love is a participation in this spiritual love.

Lustful Love

Diotima lists love for sports, philosophy and money as our secondary loves as compared to the highest love. Implicitly, I would also say a secondary love is the kind of love that seeks to fulfill the sexual appetite: lust. It is fascinating that in the *Phaedrus* Socrates gives a critique on lust. Socrates basically says if you let lust take its course it is going to lead to outrageous actions, it is going to lead to sexual assault. Because the end result of lust is violence. Violence is lust taken to its extreme.

The end result of lust

This country abolished the production code for movies in 1965 and essentially allowed pornography to be shown in the major movie theatres. The violent crime rate subsequently went up so high, especially that of sexual assault, that by 1975 lawmakers realized that they had to get pornography out of the mainstream theaters again. They knew there is a relationship between pornography and violence against women. Our police officers are not stupid. Several times in my life I have spoken with police officers who have had to deal with violent crimes like sexual assault. They say when there has been a violent sexual crime against a woman, it is almost a guarantee that pornography is involved in the perpetrator's life in almost 100 percent of the cases.

If you want to get violence against women under control, stop showing pornography or soft core porn to young men. Tell women not to dress provocatively. Get pornography filters on your computers on the campus. These are the practical ways to help stop violence against women.

There are some feminists who connect lust and violence in a backhanded way but at least they come to the truth. Catherine MacKinnon, a radical feminist in southern Indiana, says that pornography leads to sexual assault and violence. For this reason she is an advocate of putting limits on the production, sale, and distribution of pornography. She understands its harmful effects on women by the way that it leads men to see women in a particular undignified way.

Procreative love

Diotima, after critiquing lust, offers a description of true love. True love is the eternal possession of the truly good. True love gives birth to beautiful things, the most beautiful thing being beauty in another soul. In other words, true love is reproductive. But it is reproductive in a much more spiritual way than we commonly think.

One obvious example of reproductive love is the true unity between two married people. The healthy marriage relationship is not a bargain of lust, it is a self-sacrificing love between a man and a woman that leads to children. The couple engages in actions, within the context of marriage, that lead to reproduction that helps preserve the species. This is neither the highest nor the second highest; this is the third highest form of love—the unitive love between a man and a woman that is also procreative.

Diotima says "Some people seek this kind of love through the family. Cities, houses and customs should all try to protect this kind of love."

Virginal love

But Diotima says there is a higher love than the reproductive love of marriage. There is a kind of love that leads to the protection of families, cities and houses. The children that it gives rise to are spiritual children—children of virtue. This is virginal love of the Divine, the true unitive love between people. The children that it gives rise to are not physical children but spiritual children of virtue. The virtuous person will first and foremost love and care for his own body. If he is living the highest love he will treat all other bodies as if he were a brother to them and he will ultimately see that the highest beauty in each soul is its virtues, not its body.

Custom is honoring love. It governs the family or society. If someone is truly living virtue he will love the laws that lead to virtue. He will love the customs and the education that will help everybody to love in this way. He will realize that beauty is not in gold or clothing, or boys or food or drink.

It may sound funny but it makes sense. In the Netherlands this summer a political party got recognized as a legitimate party. I am not sure of the name, but perhaps it is even called the Pedophile Party. I know a lawyer in Massachusetts who is very much involved in opposing same-sex marriage and he says, "If you talk to these people in the courtroom or in the coffee shop they will tell you that their goal is not same-sex marriage. Their goal is to eliminate the families and any hierarchical institution. Same-sex marriage is one step towards eliminating the family."

Ultimately the same-sex marriage activists are anarchists. They want to destroy any institution that, in their eyes, perpetuates inequality. Families and churches are the last two things that perpetuate inequality. They are as evil to an anarchist as patriarchy is to a revolutionary.

Diotima's teachings and the Church

What Diotima teaches Socrates is the basic teaching of the Catholic Church as well, with respect to love, dating and marriage. The great encyclical, *Humanae Vitae*, which came out in 1968, says there are two aspects of love—a unitive aspect and a procreative aspect.

The highest form of love is unitive love in which the man and woman want to give themselves to God and sacrifice themselves for each other so that they can be the protectors of the family, the city and the Church. The second highest form of love is procreative love, where the man and the woman within the marriage love each other and are open to children in every action they do. Any other kind of love is a false or pseudo imitation of true love.

Man and woman in a family

Although portrayed by feminists to be so, patriarchy is not men sexually dominating women. There is another speech in the *Phaedrus* where this kind of relationship is presented—a man just dominating a woman, tyrannizing her, turning her into a sex slave.

Socrates is critical of this. He says that ultimately man and woman are equal partners. Each person has a particular mission to fulfill. Also, both have to fulfill their mission for the family as a whole first. If they do not, the family is going to fall apart.

It just so happens that oftentimes the woman runs 90 percent of the things in the house even if she is a feminist. There is always "more or less" in these sayings and there are always exceptions, but the man's role in the marriage is to more or less be the protector and to give a kind of overall direction to the family. He protects the family in the house from the dangers of the outside world. For instance, he protects his daughters from unruly high-school boys.

I was talking to my mother the other day about this. My mother said she read Ephesians Chapter 5 in her women's Bible study. This passages suggests that it is good for women to submit to their husbands and that husbands should love their wives. This passage upset several of the ladies. My mother grew up in the 1960s when everybody rejected that passage. She herself rejected it for 30 years. Now she says, "All of us older women admitted that it was right. We all admitted to it. We learned the hard way. A lot of us had to go through divorces, unhappy marriages, and a lot of instability in our lives to finally learn the truth of that statement."

A student of mine once presented an interesting take on this passage. She suggested that in that statement St. Paul is asking each person in the marriage to do the thing that is hardest for him or her to do. It is very hard for a man to truly love his wife as an equal. A man generally wants to dominate his wife and treat her as a sex object for his pleasure. Likewise, it is hard for a woman to submit to her husband. She already runs about 90 percent of the operation anyway. It is so easy to want to control the remaining 10 percent.

One of the biggest problems in marriages is that men who are unformed, in general, want to get women to do kinky things; things that are immoral. That gives men a sense of dominance—an animal-like dominance. Women oftentimes do not want to do those things but they subject themselves to men in the wrong way. They subject themselves to these things and they do not subject themselves to the things they should.

Very rarely do women dominate men sexually, but it does happen in some cases. It can happen especially because in our culture it is being promoted right now. A lot of guys have become so effeminate that they let themselves be dominated. And you also have to look at the difference between what might be happening during courtship versus what might have actually happened in a marriage.

Guidelines for relationships with women

We have lots of customs that are designed basically to protect people or to enable people to train themselves to grow in virtue so that they can learn how to love in the right way. I know that a lot of these customs seem outrageous right now and a lot of us can say, "Oh, I cannot live like that . . . I am never going to live like that . . . I have never seen anybody live like that." But these are the customs that helped protect marital love by preparing us for it or for protecting one's marriage; or if God asks us for more than marriage, then to be ready for that.

Dating

First, when you start dating a girl you must realize that it is courtship, and that it could lead to marriage. Second, it is always good to use precaution in dating girls, knowing that you are a man—knowing that you have concupiscence, and if it is not moderated, you will act like an animal.

You are more likely to become an animal when you are alone in a room with a girl than not. So it is good to avoid occasions when you are alone in a room with a girl. If you have to be alone in a room with a girl, keep the door open. That just makes common sense. Again, one of my students commented that some girls are so aggressive that they do not wait till the door is closed. My advice to you then is to stay out of the room.

I remember I was told this when I was a freshman in college. You could go to a very busy restaurant and have a very private conversation with someone because there is so much noise that no one really hears what you are saying.

So if you want to have a serious conversation the best place to do it with a girl would be a busy restaurant, not in a room alone. Private conversation alone in a room can become emotional, then from emotions there are tears, then there is hugging and so on.

Furthermore, this is where your good manners that you learned earlier comes in handy. It is good to make the effort, to struggle to treat women with refinement. Open doors for them. Call them on the phone. Buy them flowers. Send them notes. Don't tease them or interrupt them. Learn how to listen to them. Apparently, men have two bad habits in the way that they deal with women. They tend not to listen to them, and they also tend to interrupt them and tease them in all the wrong ways, basically making them feel terrible about themselves. So, something as simple as treating a young lady with refinement, and listening to her can be a great preparation for how you will treat your wife when you are married.

Dress

It is also good for men to correct women in how they dress. It will not go down real well, but take the lead. Many fathers can speak of the difficulties of doing this with their wives and daughters. Brothers can also do this, delicately, with their sisters. No matter how you say it, there is going to be a bad reaction, but the one point of leadership is if you get an initial negative reaction does not mean that the behavior will not change.

Even if girls are poorly dressed, do not gawk at them. We should be very careful about our gaze. This is something that girls notice all the time. They notice how you look at them. If you kind of look at them in a lustful, disrespectful way they notice that, and thoroughly lose respect for you.

You may ask, "Why do women dress like that? What is the point?" First, girls get caught up in fashion. Also, girls do not really realize, until they are about 35, the effect they have on men.

Sometimes I feel that men think that girls are men who wear dresses. Girls in turn think that men are girls who wear pants. We all tend to misunderstand that ultimately men are much more dominated by their sexual desires. Women tend to be more dominated by relationships.

Daughters

When you become the father of the family, one of your jobs as a father is to protect your daughters from becoming promiscuous. You are doing this to protect them against harming themselves. The primary way you do that is by loving your wife in a real way. You also do that by holding your wife and your daughters to very high standards as far as dress and modesty are concerned.

When your daughter gets to know a guy, you get to know the guy and if you think the guy is no good, you do not let her see the guy. In the way you let your daughter dress and date, you are letting her project an image of herself to the world. Your daughter expects this protection from you when you are a father. In fact, over time if you do not do it your daughter will lose respect for you. If you do it, your daughter eventually will have respect for you—although she will probably make it hard in the moment.

That is just the nature of the relationship. But that is the point. A daughter wants the man to be a man, to be the leader, to set the limits and guidelines, even if she complains and moans about it.

Be a Leader with Conviction

This is why leadership is also important when you are a husband. Women do determine what happens in about 90 percent of the things, so it is important that you choose your battles. Choose the right battles. Do not bend enough, do not capitulate. Even if the struggle seems hopeless keep at it.

However, there is always a right and a wrong way to lead. I am not saying be dictatorial, but I think what women want is conviction—confidence that you have moral standards and will not bend on your moral standards.

There is a way in which male/ female dynamics can cause men and women to play off each other to destroy each other. There is also a way that they can play off each other to lead each other to not so good ends. Then, there is also some point when they can lead each other to good.

If some women do realize their bad effect on guys and do nothing about it then they are corrupt. We should stay away from them. There are girls who are seducers.

There might be girls who are alcoholics or who might have some sort of a serious mental disorder and who become very promiscuous. In those cases their disease has gotten control over them and they might not indulge in such behavior unless somehow things got out of control.

There are also other girls who appear to be very good but in their hearts they are really little seductresses. Appearances can sometimes be deceiving. But at the same time you have to judge a little bit based on appearances to be safe.

Even if you want to be friends with a girl, take the precautions that I have mentioned to protect yourself from falling into sexual sin.

Questions and Answers

Here are some questions my students have asked me about relationships, and my replies to them:

Q: I have a friend who had started seeing one girl exclusively. They said that they were not serious, but then, all of a sudden, they started getting very intimate with each other. The problem is, it happened so fast. Then very quickly, they ended up in what seemed to be almost violent arguments with each other. It seems to be that if a guy and a girl get intimate too quickly they actually have a thin relationship.

A: That is a very good observation. There is more at stake in the male-female relationship than intimacy itself. That is why their relationship came to an end. When dating, ultimately the relationship either advances to marriage or it does not really advance.

Q: How could you just be friends with a female? Brotherly love ends at a point.

A: While talking about friendship between men and women, Francis de Sales comments that "One of the most dangerous friendships is the friendship of fondness between a man and a woman." That is the friendship where the two are friends and they say they are just friends. And they say there is nothing going on between them. These friendships can go on for several years. There are two dangerous things about these friendships. First, each soul gets stifled from growing in virtue, because they are so needy on each other's feelings that neither one of them matures. They do not establish the social relationships they should be establishing with other men or other women. Secondly, the end towards which these friendships are often progressing is sinful.

A: You may disagree with me and say that you have a lot of female friends who are practically your sisters. I agree, but it would be weird when you are married to have all those friends. Then you cannot say, "They are my sisters." Your wife will not tolerate that.

If you err too much on the side of just having female friends, it will be an obstacle to developing healthy friendships with males.

I have known a lot of guys here at the University over the years. When we start to have a heart-to-heart conversation guys say that their only real friend is a girl. I see this phenomenon even at universities that still have a competitive sports culture. One of the problems in a society like ours is that there are very few friends that we can really genuinely say are our friends. This is so because we do not even know what a friendship based on virtue is. We are not habituated to expect it. We are not educated to expect it. We are not habituated to engage in it.

What we understand of friendship is often friendship based on convenience, pleasure, efficiency or utility. A lot of other guys will say, "I know a lot of other guys," but in my own experience there are not a lot of other guys who have said to me, "These three guys are my best friends," and the friendships are based on virtue.

Q: Guys usually do not lie to each other. We do not have ulterior motives. If I do not like you I am not going to say you are my best friend.

That is true. It is a sociological fact. Priests always tell me the same thing. When they give talks, there are always certain talks that make the audiences' heads go down in shame. Usually if it is a male audience and he gives a talk on chastity or purity or pornography, the males' heads would go down. If he gives the same talk to women their heads do not go down. But if he gives a talk to them on charity, justice or holding your tongue and not gossiping, all their heads go down. In other words, men and women are built differently. Women's faults tend more to be more in the relationship area, whereas our faults tend more to be in other areas.

Of course, sexual attraction makes the big difference. There is an interest there because there is the end of marriage. And at some level it is a possibility.

CHAPTER TEN

" A ND IF THE tradition of the virtues was able to survive the horrors of the last dark ages, we are not entirely without grounds for hope. This time however the barbarians are not waiting beyond the frontiers; they have been governing us for quite some time. And it is our lack of consciousness of this that constitutes part of our predicament. We are not waiting for a Godot, but for another—doubtless very different—St. Benedict." Alasdair MacIntyre, *After Virtue*

History of the modern university

We've briefly discussed 1968, and we've discussed Animal House. It's clear that the modern university is not the 5ᵗʰ century BC Athenian Academy. But hopefully, at this point in the book, a reader could see how discussions that went on during the heyday of Ancient Athens might have some relevance to those of us immersed in the modern world and the research universities and liberal arts colleges that are the educators of the modern citizen. And so, I would like to look more closely at the modern university and at least one important part of the mentality that makes it function the way that it does. In that way, we can start trying to live virtue and educate our souls, realizing that we too, like the first followers of Socrates or like the first Christians, might find ourselves in a difficult environment. But, the environment can no longer be an excuse. We need to understand the environment in order to know what we are dealing with, not to make excuses. As Socrates said when he was dying, "If you do not live what we have been talking about here then you are all fools." Don't be a fool. *Start living it.*

Voltaire's model for revolution

The best way to understand the modern university is to examine the life of the French Enlightenment philosopher Voltaire; in particular, his plan for fostering first and foremost a cultural revolution, and then a violent revolution, in France in particular, and in the West or Europe in general. This section is based on letters written by Voltaire to his associates. In the context of Voltaire, I'll discuss Nietzsche and a mentality that predominates in the 20th Century, because this mentality carries through on the mentality with which Voltaire began his project.

Voltaire made a vow to crush the Church when he was 12 years old. In a certain sense, one could say that he was an ambitious young man. The goal of his life, he says, became to *"Ecrasez L'infame!,"* to crush the Church. *L'infame* was the church because it stifled the passions and freedom of men. When he was in his 20s he thought that within 50 years he could get a revolution going in Europe. This was in the 1720s. He gave himself a project. This was more than an ambitious engineering project—it was to crush the Church. One way to do that would be to get a revolution going in France. And it was in this context that he conceived of the French Revolution.

The scheme for cultural revolution, especially in the field of education and culture, pretty much follows the Voltairian model; though oftentimes not in as explicit terms as Voltaire articulated. If you push a lot of modern educators to their extremes you will see that he is their model.

Voltaire realized that you cannot just foment a violent revolution. Before having a violent revolution you have to have a cultural revolution, because there are actions that are part of a violent revolution, like killing Christians, that could never be carried out in times when a healthy social order is in place. So, a cultural revolution is necessary to subvert or alter the social order so that certain acts of violence, previously unacceptable, become acceptable. So he came up with a formula for a cultural revolution.

According to this formula, the first thing you have to do is you have to get rid of the religious orders, because Voltaire saw that religious orders were the defense of morality and society; they were also the defense of things like marriage and the family. They were a source of order—the religious orders were the best defense that the Church had.

Pornographic assault on France

Voltaire also saw that one way to start breaking down a culture was to inundate it with pornography over a long period of time. Pornography tends to do two things to men. It leads them to take pleasure in more and more violent actions or it weakens their wills. Either way, they feel guilty and resentful at what they are doing to themselves. So, men who acquire the bad habits associated with this literature will be prime targets for instigating a revolution, or can be counted on to do nothing against it when it starts. England, which was trying to bring about something like the Glorious Revolution in France, for example, sent its radicals to the Netherlands or Belgium, where they would set up radical publishing houses. From Belgium, the pornographers would use the mail to inundate France with their materials.

Voltaire as a young man adopted ideas that harmonized well with the English project of getting a revolution going in France. He traveled to England in the 1720s and at that point he became an agent of the English government, trying to help bring about a cultural and political revolution in the French regime. What he was doing in France was certainly in sync with what the English government was trying to do, as far as fostering a cultural and even a violent revolution in France.

As said before, the English sent their radicals to Netherlands from where they sent pornography *en masse* down into France. The Netherlands and Belgium had relatively liberal publication laws. The strategy was to try to use legal ways to weaken the Church and at the same time send pornography down into France as a way of corrupting the morals of the people over time.

This effort at widespread distribution of pornography was pretty bad in the 17th century, and got worse in the France of the 18th century. By the eve of the French Revolution, the Palais Royale in Paris was a cesspool of pornographic literature. It is also the part of Paris from which flowed the radical words and deeds that led to the French Revolution. France has been subject to vicious pornographic campaigns for almost the last 300 years now. That had its effect on its culture.

Getting rid of the religious orders

Voltaire saw that religious orders were the bulwark of Universities. The religious orders tended to enable universities to uphold very high standards on what was reasonable, what was allowable, what was rational and so forth. Voltaire also saw that the Jesuits were the staunchest amongst all the religious orders in defending the rights of the Church at universities and in public life. He reasoned that if they fell, all the other religious orders would fall as well.

So he and his associates worked to get as many Jesuits thrown out of the European countries as possible. Then they also worked to get the orders suppressed. They were effective in doing that. Certainly by the 1770s the Jesuits were suppressed as an order and the only place they existed any more was in Russia, due to Catherine the Great. Catherine the Great did not want to suppress them as they were the only people educating the Russian barbarians that she wanted to modernize.

The next thing that Voltaire said was, "*We have to take over the university.*" Another way that Voltaire thought of getting rid of the religious orders was by convincing Catholics that they should delay the vocations of their children. He said, "All we have to do is to convince good Catholics to start arguing that their children should put off the question of their vocation until they are 21, or even earlier, maybe 19. By that time most young people would do something that would lead them to think they could never have a vocation to serve God in a serious way."

That was one of the ways he tried to decrease the numbers of the orders by getting the Catholics themselves to accept the idea that young people should delay making important life choices until they are 21 or 22. By and large he succeeded in his efforts. Perhaps one of the reasons for a dearth of vocations in Western countries is that we are afraid to challenge young people from the time they are 14 or 16 to think about what God might want them to do with their lives. Perhaps if we wish to resolve this crisis of vocations, we should challenge ourselves from the time we are 14, 16, or 18 to think and pray about what God is asking us to do with our lives.

Taking over the universities

After harassing the Jesuits and then weakening the number of young Catholics who were willing to enter the religious orders, he then said, "*We have to get the orders out of the university.*" To do so he proposed using the doctrine of toleration as a pretext for getting Protestants and then Jansenists,[1] followed by atheists, into the universities.

JEFFREY J. LANGAN

Voltaire argued that we have to use the doctrine of toleration to get an atheist into the universities, since toleration means we should be open to all different positions. He said that once they got an atheist into the universities, that atheist could start to use blackmail, gossip and slander campaigns to make life so uncomfortable for the Catholics that they would all want to leave. He says, "We atheists, we can always ally ourselves with the Jansenists and the Protestants to kick the Catholics out. Once we do that, once you have just a generation of Protestantism and Jansenism, the next generation would usually be atheist." If you have 20 to 40 years of Jansenism and Protestantism, their intellectual children will most likely be atheist.

Voltaire said that the Protestants and the atheists will naturally form an alliance against the Catholics in most disciplines. We have seen this even in modern Catholic universities where in the 1970s they would hire a lot of modern Protestant philosophers, who in hiring and making tenure decisions would ally themselves with atheists against the Catholics. They would do this because in many ways both agree that faith and reason are incompatible. If you are a Protestant, and your philosophy leads to nothingness, that makes your act of faith all the greater—faith is an act in the face of irrationality.

In contrast, traditionally the Catholic view is more oriented towards there being some kind of harmony between faith and reason. Ultimately, my active faith is still an active faith, but it is not completely irrational either. It is not based on some irrational act in an abyss. Voltaire in his letters said that, "Once we get the serious Catholics out of the universities then we can let back in Catholics who are compromisers." The compromisers are either corrupt or they are people who can easily be compromised or persuaded because they are not smart enough to understand positions and doctrines that go against their own. This "dumbing down" also implies getting the religious academics out of the university. Voltaire opined that once this was done, the stage might be set for a more violent revolution, as the revolutionaries would very easily be able to eliminate the influence of the Church on society. Note that it was very easy for him to get control of other means of culture such as the theatre.

One of Voltaire's friends was the King of Prussia. In one of his letters to Voltaire, Frederick asked: Can I start killing the Catholics now? Can I do it now? Can I do it now? And Voltaire responded: No, no, no, wait. You have to wait. You cannot start killing the Catholics straight away. You have to wait until they are weak enough culturally so that you can just slaughter them and no one will care anymore. In retrospect, this exchange is somewhat funny. But, at the same time, it is disturbing. At a recent conference on the French Revolution and the Enlightenment, one of the participants, in defending Immanuel Kant's approval of the assassination of priests and nuns during the Revolution, commented, "it is good for priests to be chastised every now and then." Voltaire's thought is not so foreign to us.

By the early 1780s, Voltaire realized that the Revolution he had worked for his entire life was about to happen. The cultural foundation was set. It was only a matter of time before a great revolution swept through France.

The kind of cultural warfare envisioned by Voltaire became part of the practice of the French Revolution. I was in Marseilles a couple of summers ago, studying the French Revolution there. Every spring there, the revolutionaries would have some sort of a blasphemous or vulgar, or quasi-pornographic play performed in February and March. The basic model of the revolution is that once people's morality is weakened then all you have to do to incite the mob is to introduce them to pornography or to something that is vulgar or blasphemous. At that point, they will become enraged because their passions will start to take control of them. Then it would be easy to control them. If you are smart enough you can actually control them to go after the government or the King or their priest. As they are controlled by their passions, you can manipulate their passions to suggest to them who their real enemy is.

Kulturkampf

In the French Revolution the revolutionaries began to distinguish between cultural revolution and violent revolution. Voltaire's model became a fast-forward thing; it was the model that Nietzsche adopted, and then Bismarck in Germany in the 19th century, in establishing universities. There is a famous story about a chair at a German university that was open, as a Catholic professor was retiring. Bismarck fought tooth and nail behind the scenes to make sure that another Catholic did not replace him. The person who had that chair would promote research. He wanted someone in that chair who promoted research *and* would be pro-German nation, and felt that a Catholic would not do that.

Incidentally, Bismarck coined the word *Kulturkampf* or "culture war" to indicate how he was going to eliminate the influence of the Catholics in Germany. He saw that the obstacle to Prussia gaining dominance in Germany was the Catholics. *Kulturkampf* was a way of eliminating the cultural and political influence of Catholics—first in the universities, then in political society, then in the country as a whole.

By the end of the 19th century, especially in France and Germany, the cultural war was very successful. The Catholics who comprised 80 to 90 percent of the population of areas like Bavaria and the Lower Rhine would only have maybe ten percent representation in the universities. The *Kulturkampf* was very successful in getting all the Catholics out of the intellectual life of the country because this was the way of getting them out of the cultural life of the country.

Even today, when we speak of free speech or a play on campus or academic freedom and such, it is important to understand it in context, not simply as an individual event. We should ask questions such as: *Where does this play stand? What is going on here, as far as the overall history of the West? What do the different groups really represent, as far as the history of the West goes?*

The German university that Bismarck started and popularized in the 19th century was often times predicated on this ideal: "We have to found a science which does not appeal to anything either philosophically or theologically." Many of the social sciences in the 19th century were founded on the same ideal. They would not in any way go along with what has traditionally been taught about morality in the Church or in the West.

Many universities were founded on this explicit condition of having sciences that would not appeal at all to traditional values. Many Classics departments in the United States in the late 19th and early 20th century that involved the study of Latin and Greek purposely eliminated Aristotle and Plato from the Classics—because their writings are too compatible with Catholic morality.

The revolution in America's universities

Many of America's universities, particularly almost all the research universities such as Michigan, Berkeley, Wisconsin, Michigan State, Nebraska or Texas, are founded on the model of the German universities of the 19th century. They want to develop sciences that they can use as a club against, or to get around, the norms of traditional morality.

This is further compounded by the fact that many of the German intellectuals are the same ones that built up the Bismarckian state that led to the World War I, or the conditions that led to the Nazi state that led to World War II, or what led to Communist Russia, or what pretty much led to socialist France—all of the havoc that was wreaked on Europe in the twentieth century. Many of these intellectuals were the first to leave Europe in the 1930s and 1940s when things got bad.

This is a classic way to understand the intellectuals of the last 200 years. They have all these crazy ideas, they get countries to implement their ideas, the countries or societies go berserk and then the intellectuals leave. That is a typical trope of an intellectual. They do all sorts of things that ruin people's lives because people take them seriously. They take no responsibility for the harm they have caused to people, and they just go somewhere else.

What basically happened is that they followed this Voltairian model in humanities and science in the 19th and 20th centuries. They made it extreme and refined it one way or another. But this is the model that exists.

In most Catholic universities in this country from the 1950s to the 1970s, most Catholic intellectuals were kicked out in the same way as Voltaire modeled it back in the 18th century. First Catholic universities have to accept the doctrine of tolerance and let in an atheist or a Protestant. Before you know it, the atheists and the Protestants are uniting with one another to kick out the Catholics. Then you have the whole problem of the Catholics who lost their faith in the 1970s. They became the compromising Catholics that Voltaire describes, who allied themselves with the other group in order to always keep the Catholics down.

Revolution in our times

In 1998, I was staying at a residence in Paris watching a documentary about Daniel Cohn-Bendit and the revolution of 1968. Daniel Cohn-Bendit was a Communist spy from East Germany who came to France in the 1950s. His goal was to try to get a violent revolution going in the West.

This is not anything that I did secret research to discover. This was what was being said explicitly on French national television. So this is approved discourse. The only public discourse that is allowed in France anymore is modern, subversive, revolutionary discourse.

And the idea that Voltaire proposed but Nietzsche perfected was to go from cultural revolution to violent revolution you wear whatever mask you need to wear at that time, so that people will accept you. If the mask you need to wear is one of a Civil Rights activist or a cultural revolutionary, that is what you do. You then take the mask off and become a violent revolutionary when the moment is right. Bendit-Cohn said that he and his associates thought from the 1950s until 1972 that the time was ripe for fermenting a violent revolution in the West. If we got a violent revolution in the West going we could create universal communist societies."

The communists started making all these contacts, which they had because of all their other buddies who had come to the US in the 1930s and 1940s. So they had contacts between the socialists, the universities of Europe and universities of the United States. In the 1950s and 1960s they made contacts at New York University, Cornell, Columbia, Berkeley, Wisconsin—throughout the US. Sometime in the mid-1960s they decided to shoot for 1968 and use the Vietnam War as their pretext to get the revolution going. They presented themselves as being against the war, as trying to get a revolution going against those societies which allowed for this. They were also promoting the hippie communes, the sexual revolution, just as Voltaire did with pornography in the 18th century in France. This was all a way for laying the ground for the violent revolution.

In 1968, the Church released *Humanae Vitae*. All the so-called Catholic theologians and philosophers had been organizing for three years in advance of its release, to have an organized public relations campaign to cause disinformation about what the Pope was going to teach in *Humanae Vitae*. When it came out they took out an advertisement in the *New York Times* and held protests on the steps of buildings in Washington. They got huge press coverage. They were supremely media savvy. They ran a massive campaign of disinformation to cause confusion about what the Pope was teaching in *Humanae Vitae*.

They did this to foster a revolutionary attitude against the visible Church. They were like the Jansenists. "The visible church is corrupt. We are the spirit. We are the people." A visitor to our Center said, "Gosh I remember in '68 being down there in Texas hand in hand with all my buddies, singing *We are one in the Spirit*, against the Bishop." *We are the invisible Church against the visible Church.* He then reminded me what strange and crazy times were those years, '68 to '72!

In the late 1960s the revolutionaries broke the Hollywood production code and allowed pornography to be distributed in all the theaters. I was in Germany in 2004 and met some psychologists who were leaders in the various cities in Germany. The fascinating thing is that these guys said the same thing that Daniel Cohn-Bendit said. They said, "Oh *ja*, when I was in high school my communist operative who was working with me got me to do two things that made me a violent revolutionary. He got me to masturbate and got me to start hating my father. Once that happened I was committed to violent revolution." The man said the exact same thing as Daniel Cohn-Bendit: "From about 1968 to 1972 we were trying to get the violent revolution going. But sometime in 1972 we realized it was not going to work. So we decided that we were going to put on the mask of being pacifists and cultural revolutionaries."

Daniel Cohn-Bendit said this on public TV in France! Remember, the people in France glorify the revolution: "Oh yes! The Revolution!"

The interviewer asks Daniel Cohn-Bendit, "So is that what has been going on in the West for the last 20 or 25 years or so?" He replies, "*Ja*, in all of our networks we have been spreading cultural revolution through the institutions."

In the United States, after 1989, when the Berlin Wall fell and Communism fell, all the Marxists began calling themselves post-modernists. They did not change their beliefs at all. They just realized they could not promote their beliefs by calling themselves Marxists any more. It would not be tolerated. So they called themselves post-modernists instead.

There is a professor here on campus who was invited by the so-called conservative Catholics to have a discussion with them years ago. I was invited as well, and I had just started doing some research on the French Revolution. So we were at dinner. I was talking to this Professor. He is an older man of about 70. Everybody knows him as a conservative. He asked me what I was working on. I replied, "Well, I am starting a research project on the French

Revolution." His eyes lit up. "Ah! The French Revolution! Weren't those great times?" I said, "Actually I am doing some research on various reactions to the French Revolution, about people who were somehow affected by it." He said, "Yes, the people were affected. It was so great. You should study Herder. He was a philosopher, who went to fight in the streets of Paris. You should study Hegel. He celebrated the first anniversary of the revolution with his buddies. They planted a liberty tree in Germany because they were great advocates."

I realized that this man was a fan of the French Revolution. He thought it was a great thing. He is desirous of another French Revolution. And he is supposedly the conservative that they are inviting for their little Catholic book discussion. Something is wrong here!

A lot of people, especially in intellectual life, are just huge advocates of the revolution. They like this idea of a revolution that overturns society, oftentimes because they do not have to suffer the effects of it. They can just theorize about it. It has great theoretical benefits.

How to change things

A student asked me, "How would you turn back the revolution in the universities?"

My personal view as far as how to change things coincides with that of the Pope. Last year, when he was elected, the Pope said, "I have no plan, my only plan is sanctity." Perhaps it is enough that to begin with, we speak the truth about what has got us to where we are now. That, at least, is a start. If someone is a drug addict or an alcoholic, the first thing he or she needs to do is to admit the truth about his or her situation. Often, the parents or family are blind to the reality of what is going on. Even if they do know, it is not necessarily by a direct confrontation that they can convince the sick person to seek help. The person has to come to see it on his own, hopefully sooner rather than later. So, just knowing the story can be a start.

It sounds almost innocuous, but it is people who are truly committed to sanctity, truly committed to living the virtues and being very united with Christ, who will foster change. These are the people who, whatever decisions they have to make, are not going to think about what men think about these decisions. They will think more about what God thinks about their decisions.

The second thing is that we have to stop thinking that our goal is to become lawyers and doctors. We have to start thinking that our goal is to become educators. Your goal should be to get your Ph.D. in something. Even if you do not become a Ph.D., you must think of going into journalism or the media. We have to have more of a willingness and even know that this might be a kind of martyrdom—not a martyrdom like getting your head chopped off, but knowing that by going into one of these professions you might live a kind of martyrdom in your life. Your life might just end up being an example some two hundred years later that some Catholic happens to stumble upon and realizes, "Hey, this guy did it right!"

Over the break there were some guys who were watching a promotional video of the University. What was very striking to me about this promotional video was that the student they were showing was the dumb jock: "I use my hands . . . I like to use my hands and make presentations . . . I am going to be a doctor someday . . . I am majoring in political science and business right now, because you know I love to use my hands . . . If I am here for two more years, I will not even be speaking English anymore, I will just be grunting."

Then the other guy in the video was also going to be a doctor: "I am going to make a lot of . . ." I actually know some of these students. I know this is how they really think; this is not just how they think for the video.

A lot of people really say, "I want to be a doctor or lawyer, make a lot of money and live a comfortable life, and I can say I am doing a good service to the country while I am doing it." I do not disparage being a doctor or a lawyer. But, the only things that a lot of Catholic universities produce are doctors and lawyers and engineers. If your calling is to be an engineer, be an engineer. But when you have a university of 1,000 students and nearly 300 become engineers, 300 become doctors, around 400 become lawyers and three people go on to get their PhD in something, there is a disproportion there. There is something wrong with this equation. If someone has the capacity to get a PhD they should, even knowing that it might be a sacrifice. Otherwise the university is lost.

That is what you can do. These are things we could pray for. We should pray.

JEFFREY J. LANGAN

"WHAT A MAN'S virtue is capable of is not to be measured by his exceptional efforts, but by his daily life." Pascal, *Penseés* 352

The Mountain of Virtue

Usually, when a philosophy professor or history professor describes in an accurate way the change in ideas and culture over the past 200 years, at least some students start to despair, asking the question, "What can I do? What can I do to start changing things?" One answer: The "mountain of virtue."

Students I respect tell me that they realize in retrospect that the best thing that they could have done in their four years at the university is that they could have started to learn how to live virtue; not only how to love virtue, but to seriously start living it.

When you are young and dominated by your passions (or your passions are strong), and your intellect is a little bit more mature than the rest of you. It is very easy to think that we know the truth or that we have the right ideas, but we inevitably fail to put them into effect, fail to start living them.

The "mountain of virtue" is the countermeasure. Ascending the mountain of virtue is something that you can start to do now in order to change society in the long run. Who are the men who will ultimately change our society? Men who are first and foremost dedicated to discovering who God is, what the nature of God is, and how to live in a way that is consistent with the nature of God. The men who will change our society are the men who become friends with God. Because they become friends with God, they see all of creation and other people as God does. Agents of change will be men who want to befriend other men as God does, and introduce them to God.

Origin of the "mountain"

Several years ago a basketball coach, Will, visited here. He told us his story of how he had decided as a junior in college to become a basketball coach, and why, after coaching for many years as a college coach, he decided to become a high school coach. This decision had to do with what turned out to be his initial reason for being a coach in the first place.

Will coached at the college level for many years at places like Evansville and Butler. At one point he went to Xavier in Cincinnati. But he realized at some point in his life that the reason he went into coaching was that he was really interested in teaching young men virtue and how to live virtue. He realized that he could not really lay the foundation for virtue in a young man's soul at the college level. Oftentimes at the college level, the players were already set in which way they wanted to go in life. So he thought that one of the best ways to teach virtue to students would be to teach at the high school level. He left Xavier and got a job as a basketball coach at a high school in Chicago.

He switched from college coaching to high school coaching after reflecting on the reasons why he became a coach in the first place. Will told us of the time when as a college student he paid his way to go to the national meeting of the Association of College Basketball Coaches. When he went to this meeting he was the only college student there among all these coaches. One of the main speakers was John Wooden, the great coach of the 1960s and 1970s whose team won ten NCAA Championships in 12 seasons, including one run of seven years. His teams had four undefeated seasons. If you know something about college basketball, you know that these numbers are unparalleled and a sign of true excellence, even if it is only on the basketball court. Of course, Will, being an idealistic junior in college who wanted to become the next John Wooden, wanted to get Wooden's secret to success at a young age. At the end of the conferences Will went up to Wooden and asked, "What is the secret of your success?" Wooden said "Write me a letter and I will tell you." As soon as Will got home, he sent a letter to Wooden and eagerly awaited a response. Who would not want to know the secret of success? Wooden wrote back and simply sent him one sheet of paper with a pyramid on it. On the pyramid were written a bunch of virtues.

In an accompanying note, Wooden explained to Will, "I evaluate all of my teams based on how they make progress in relation to this pyramid. And it is not my teams that win the National Championships that I consider necessarily the most successful teams. It is the teams that really make the most progress with respect to this pyramid that I consider my best teams. Everyday I look at my pyramid and I try to ask myself how I can improve my team; and how I can improve myself with respect to this pyramid."

When I saw Wooden's pyramid, I thought it was a good idea. I also thought that a similar pyramid could be made not just for basketball, but for living one's life. What I am giving you is not the same pyramid that Wooden gave Will. He gave me a photocopy of what Wooden gave to him. I looked at it and said to myself, "I bet you we at the Center can come up with a pyramid, not just for success, but for virtue, based on our knowledge of college students. We have been around at the University for14 years or so, and can build a pyramid based on what people have told us, and based on our effort to live either Aristotelian or Thomistic virtues or both at the University." Ultimately I said to myself, "What would be the pyramid of virtues for a college student, for a college student looking at *all* of reality?"

And this is the pyramid I have come up with.

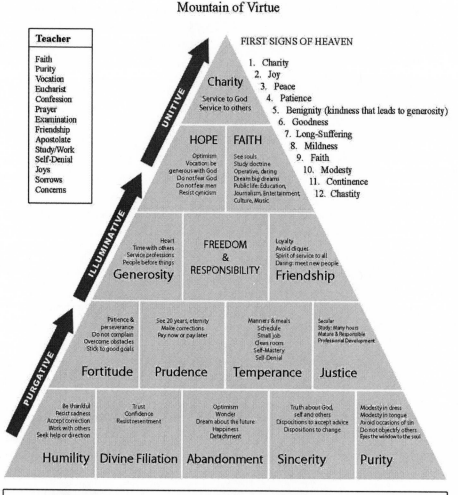

Mountain of Virtue

Teacher

Faith
Purity
Vocation
Eucharist
Confession
Prayer
Examination
Friendship
Apostolate
Study/Work
Self-Denial
Joys
Sorrows
Concerns

FIRST SIGNS OF HEAVEN

1. Charity
2. Joy
3. Peace
4. Patience
5. Benignity (kindness that leads to generosity)
6. Goodness
7. Long-Suffering
8. Mildness
9. Faith
10. Modesty
11. Continence
12. Chastity

UNITIVE

Charity
Service to God
Service to others

HOPE
Optimism
Vocation: be generous with God
Do not fear God
Do not fear men
Resist cynicism

FAITH
See souls
Study doctrine
Operative, daring
Dream big dreams
Public life: Education, Journalism, Entertainment, Culture, Music

ILLUMINATIVE

Generosity
Heart
Time with others
Service professions
People before things

FREEDOM & RESPONSIBILITY

Friendship
Loyalty
Avoid cliques
Spirit of service to all
Daring: meet new people

PURGATIVE

Fortitude
Patience & perseverance
Do not complain
Overcome obstacles
Stick to good goals

Prudence
See 20 years, eternity
Make corrections
Pay now or pay later

Temperance
Manners & meals
Schedule
Small job
Clean room
Self-Mastery
Self-Denial

Justice
Secular
Study: Many hours
Mature & Responsible
Professional Development

Humility
Be thankful
Resist sadness
Accept correction
Work with others
Seek help or direction

Divine Filiation
Trust
Confidence
Resist resentment

Abandonment
Optimism
Wonder
Dream about the future
Happiness
Detachment

Sincerity
Truth about God, self and others
Dispositions to accept advice
Dispositions to change

Purity
Modesty in dress
Modesty in tongue
Avoid occasions of sin
Do not objectify others
Eyes the window to the soul

1. Abandonment.
2. Faith in God.
3. Trust in Him.
4. Fearless examination of Conscience.
5. Confession of injustices.

6. Want to lose character defects.
7. Humbly ask God to remove them.
8. Make amends to those we have harmed.
9. Sincerely admit when we are wrong.
10. Daily Prayer to deepen our friendship with God & introduce Him to others.

Virtues on the pyramid

These are the virtues that are positioned on the bottom of the pyramid. You can find elements of these virtues, or descriptions of these, in all of Plato's dialogues on some level or another. For example, in *Alcibiades II* Socrates tries to teach Alcibiades how to have trust and confidence in the divine being, how to abandon himself to the designs of the divine being, and how to pray. Socrates seems to think that one of the first things someone does in order to put himself on the path to living virtue is to learn how to commune with or to pray to the divine being. Remember this is Socrates here. We are not talking about faith, but a necessary part of beginning the struggle to grow in human virtue as understood by a pre-Christian philosopher.

Sincerity

A fundamental challenge that Socrates lays out for starting along the path of living virtue is striving for sincerity. Sincerity is consistency between what is in your heart, what is in your thoughts, what is in your speech and what is in your deeds. The truly sincere person shows harmony between the heart, thoughts, words and deeds.

If there is any disharmony between heart, thoughts, words and deeds, then essentially this existence is a lie, because deeds betray thoughts. On a practical level it helps to find at least one person in life to whom you can be completely sincere. In fact, it is a life-long struggle to get in the habit of speaking sincerely to another person who can help you. It is so easy to lie to oneself. Then, it is a big struggle after you are sincere to change your behavior to conform to the desires of your heart, words, and speech. Or, to change whatever needs to be changed within you so that your life conforms to the truth.

My friend's observation is very true: During your college years you will either start to change your behavior to conform to your ideals or you will change your ideals to conform to your behavior. If you have high ideals of virtue, generosity, and service and you are serious about these ideals, you will, in a practical way, make your behavior conform to your ideals. If you have high ideals but you do not live them, and you behave in ways that betray or violate your ideals, over time you will start to rationalize your misbehavior. You will start to change your ideals to conform to your disorder, whatever it might be.

Humility

Another element of sincerity is the desire or the willingness to discover and to conform yourself to the truth. Part of it is humility too. The basic attitude of someone who is humble is that he thinks of himself as nothing, as being given a great gift and many talents by God, and he wants to discover the truth so that he can conform himself to the truth. He does not want to deny the truth or try to create a reality, and project his disorder onto reality.

Remember from Chapter Four: you will over time project the order or the disorder of your soul into what you do—your work, your family life and your friendships. If your soul is ordered, you will project order and charity into all of your affairs. If your soul is disordered, you will project disorder and chaos into everything you do and into society as a whole.

You cannot escape this fact. The things that you do shape your soul. All of your actions have effects. To speak unjustly, to lack temperance, to be lazy, to waste time—all of these behaviors will have effects in your life. They will influence how you act and how you see the world. So, it is important that you live temperance, justice, prudence and fortitude now. Begin to discover these virtues, what they mean. Stop doing things that violate these virtues. Try to do things that conform your behavior to these virtues. This way, you will project virtue rather than vice into your friendships, your work, and the institutions of society.

The vulgar or lower standards, or the disordered standards of the world, could very easily overtake and consume ordinary people. They will, unless you, the leaders, start to live virtue, thus creating the environment that will help pull many people up to higher standards of living. In a sense, if leaders ascend the mountain of virtue it will help undo the cultural and violent revolution.

If someone learns how to grow in virtue, to discover the truth, and to conform his soul to the truth, then when he is participating in the institutions of society, he will project into those institutions the order that is in his soul.

All these virtues on this bottom row here are the first steps, the baby steps. The nice thing about growing in virtue is that it is just like playing a sport: You can always go back to the fundamentals. You also always need to go back to the fundamentals. No matter how advanced you think you are, you always need to go back and revisit the fundamentals.

The four cardinal virtues

When someone starts to live the struggle of acquiring virtue, he will start to manifest in his life the four cardinal virtues. The four cardinal virtues are the hinge of all the other virtues. In fact, Plato goes on to say, and Aristotle joins him, that pretty much each of the four cardinal virtues is implicated in every action, one way or another.

Fortitude

Fortitude is *not* joining the military. I know that a lot of times men who think they are wimps or weaklings or if they need to get tough on themselves, join a boxing tournament such as the campus boxing club, or join the military. I had a friend who joined the military because he thought he needed to grow in virtue. A lot of times alcoholics do this. They think if they join the military, they will have life strict and serious enough that they will not drink anymore. However, I have met a lot of amateur boxers, football players and Army Generals who are cowards from the standpoint of the virtue of fortitude. Joining these institutions and clubs does not make you tough. Real toughness or fortitude has to do with the dispositions of your soul.

The toughness that you learn from playing a sport is a preparation for virtue, but it is not necessarily fortitude. Fortitude is sticking to what is good and true, independent of difficulties; it is overcoming difficulties or obstacles so as to stick with what is good and true.

One of the first signs of fortitude is that a person is aware of what is good. Even though it might be difficult, the person does not complain. He tries to put all his efforts into carrying out and doing what is good even though it might be daunting. All men tend to be complainers about something. Fortitude helps us to have the right approach with respect to fear, pleasures and pains. It gives us the confidence to persevere in discovering what is true and sticking to the good when difficulties arrive. It leads us to fear the right things (like offending God), and to not fear the wrong things (like losing our reputation or missing out on what is, in reality, only cheap pleasure). Fortitude is related to developing the patience necessary to overcome difficulties in order to persevere in a task once we have started it.

Prudence

Prudence is wisdom about how to live one's life. A truly prudent person sees creation as God does. He knows the right principles that guide human action and he also knows very well the circumstances he is in, and how to act in those circumstances. We often associate prudence with age, because older people have a lot of experience. But, you can be prudent from a young age.

Remember, you can either accept what is true as a young man and live it, or you can learn in the sad and harsh school of experience. This is the purpose of taking the right courses and studying when you are in college. If you get a good sense of the truths that guide morality and the richness of human experience that can be gleaned from history and literature, you will have taken the first steps in being prudent. If you were to start to take seriously and live what the Ten Commandments require, you would start to become prudent. If you were to start to use your time well so that you can really study in college, you would be prudent.

People tend to forget that the prudent person corrects things when he realizes they need to be corrected. There is an old saying, "You either pay now or you pay later." You will realize how true it is when you raise your children. I see it in the classroom all the time. The teacher might on the first day of class be easygoing with his students and the students might get good grades. They might get an easy A, but they do not learn anything. During the course of the class, the students may lose respect for the teacher because they realize they are not learning anything, even though in the moment they say they like it.

I knew a professor once who wanted good student evaluations. So, he bought the students pizza on a regular basis and watched TV with them in class. The students in the moment thought it was great, but looking back on it, they did not think they learned anything in that class. What a waste of time and money!

Looking back on their academic careers, the classes most students remember the most and feel they got the most out of are the hardest ones. They look back and realize, "That is where I learned something; that is where I got something that is worth the $40,000 a year I paid."

Whenever you are in charge, you either pay now or pay later. If you notice a problem with a child, a colleague, or someone in the office, and you do not correct it right away, it will pop up as a big problem later on.

Temperance

Temperance ultimately is harmonizing all of your passions, emotions and feelings so as to do good. One of the actual manifestations of temperance is order, both spiritual and physical.

Perhaps spiritual order is more important than physical order. Spiritual order means that you understand who you are with respect to God, your fellowmen, your family and your job.

The temperate person knows how to create the proper priorities in his life. For example, a man could be very orderly in that he keeps his office and makes his bed; but could be very disorderly in that he works 80 hours a week and is never home for his wife or children. The physical order could hide a deep spiritual disorder. A student who is very disciplined during the week so that he can get drunk on the weekends is not ordered or temperate. He is disordered.

Plato thought it was essential for young people to get up early in the morning. This is one of the first signs of temperance. A well-respected colleague of mine agrees with this. One of the signature indications that a student in college is living temperance is that he had early classes, that he takes the time to pray for ten to 15 minutes, and that he eats breakfast before he goes to class in the morning. Another sign of temperance is that the person treats his day at college as a work day, trying to get his work done by 6:00 p.m. This makes time in the evening for extra-curricular activities and for cultivating friendship with others.

Justice

Justice is giving to each what is due to him. A big part of justice is taking seriously your responsibilities as a student, father, citizen, colleague, and a man of God. A student at a university should realize that his primary job is to study. Many people have made sacrifices, including paying taxes, to help set up a university that will educate the student. The student, therefore, owes a debt to the university and society. He repays this debt by spending the time necessary to develop his intellect and to prepare himself for the upcoming adventure that is the rest of his life.

Ages of interior life

On the right side of the mountain are the words purgative, illuminative and unitive. These are the ages of the ascetical life, or the ages of the interior life. There is a kind of progression of going up the mountain here. There are different features that characterize each age of the struggle.

Purgative Stage

When you are younger and just starting out, you tend to go through what is called the purgative stage. In this stage, you feel the strong pull of your passions. The struggle to grow in virtue is difficult to understand, and it is hard to start out. It is harder to do a lot of the simple things like pray and schedule your time at this age. They cost more effort. Some of the struggles against the passions might be more violent.

The purgative stage is when the person starts to put in place the basic struggles to gain dominion over the basic passions of the soul and starts to point the soul in the right direction. Some people never get out of this stage in their lives, because they do not know how to start out or because they never even try. It is such a shame because there is so much more to life, if they were to set out to climb the mountain.

Illuminative Stage

In the second stage, the illuminative stage, many of the basic struggles of controlling the passions are not as violent. This stage is analogous to the stage when someone who plays the guitar or who plays football develops a modest proficiency in the instrument or the sport. The person has acquired a basic dominion over the passions. He begins to understand the effort it takes to grow in virtue and he engages in it with a certain ease. He is aware of the typical mistakes that he and others can make in growing in virtue and he knows how to avoid them. He also has a sense of growing in virtue, what it takes.

The passions are still there. They are always there—you can always return to the purgative stage; you can always take a step back. But the person starts to see more clearly the truth of things. He also probably starts to see more clearly very specific struggles he can engage in.

Very often the illuminative stage is like a plateau. When people learn instruments, in the first two or three years, the person can make a lot of progress. Then the person hits a plateau. There might be a long time when the person is practicing, practicing, practicing and seemingly not making much progress. In actuality the person is making progress, because he cannot get to the next stage unless he goes through this long plateau.

A friend in college played the Irish fiddle. He started playing when he was five. By the time he was seven he had proficiency. Then, he had a five to seven year period during which he did not seem to make any progress. He practiced every day, and his parents and brothers and sisters had to put up with a poor sounding young violinist. But then, one day in his teens, he started playing the fiddle with great ease. It was a delight to listen to it. He joined an Irish band. The effort had developed fruit. Growing in virtue, the effort involved, is similar to the effort and progress of my friend in learning to play the fiddle.

The illuminative stage might last from when you are 20 until you are 60. It depends on the grace that God gives you, what kind of efforts you put in and other things. But the illuminative stage is a long plateau where you see struggles, are engaging in them, and may have special insights here and there. You may have special moments in which you sense or experience more clearly the joy and happiness that comes from living virtue. But it is not the norm.

When you live the virtues that I have listed for this stage you start to recognize what true freedom is, and what responsibility is. You start to see what true generosity is and are actually generous in your behavior with others. Then you start to understand more clearly what friendship is.

Unitive Stage

The third stage is the unitive stage. In this stage you start to have special insight into the highest truths and you can live most of the virtues with a kind of facility and ease. You start to really experience real happiness, the first signs of heaven, the first signs of eternal life.

I have put the three theological virtues on the top of the mountain: faith, hope and charity. As soon as you are baptized, the theological virtues are infused in your soul. They make themselves more manifest and start to bear more fruit once you have struggled more to grow in the human virtues.

The first signs of Heaven

Finally, if you are truly trying to prepare your soul for true happiness and true good during your life, you will start to show manifestations of the first signs of heaven. That is the box in the upper right hand corner: Charity, joy, peace, patience, kindness, goodness, long suffering, mildness—or meekness as some people call it—faith, modesty, continence and chastity.

Virtues that need a teacher

On the left side of the mountain are those topics that a person talks about with his teacher or guide. If he really wants to grow in virtue, he finds an older and wiser person with whom he can speak about his struggle to grow in virtue. This person is like a coach for the soul. That is one of the reasons Plato established the Academy. I think that is the quote we have in our Academy brochure: "In a world that is going nuts," or as Plato or Socrates say in the *Republic*, "In a world that has gone crazy, it is important that we find someone who can guide our soul." And we entrust ourselves to that person; we trust their authority, that they can lead us down the path of virtue.

These things underneath the teacher on the left hand side are the typical things about which a person can start to talk to a guider of souls or a mentor of souls.

Remember, the Academy is not just an intellectual exercise. There are two aspects of the philosophical life—the moral life, which is the growth in virtues; and the intellectual life, which involves honing your intellectual powers so that you can see better the truth of things. The two are intimately related. If we fail to live the virtues, we have greater difficulty seeing the reality of things.

If we fail to see the reality of things, over time, it is harder for us to grow in the virtues. So these two aspects play off each other. A teacher or a mentor is someone who can help us objectively look at ourselves and our circumstances; and challenge us to grow in the virtues so that we can start to discover what the Divine Being is, what Providence is and what the Divine Being might be expecting of us throughout our lives.

I know that some students at two different colleges have started "Esto Vir" clubs. *Esto Vir* is Latin for "Be a Man." In these clubs the young men found a book that explains and challenges its readers to grow in virtue. These young men do something very simple. They meet each week for an hour or less. They read some points from the book, and each one tries to think of practical ways that he can live the points read. This sounds very simple, but anyone could gather together two or three friends of the same sex and try to do this.

The things I place to the left of the pyramid are the contexts or the events within which a person or a young man could start to discover how to pray, and then through his prayer start to discover how he can better live virtue. These things are faith, purity, vocation, mission or calling, participating in the Eucharist, Confession, prayer, examining our conscience, friendship (or trying to lead other souls in the same direction that we are going), our capacity to study and to work, our capacity for self-denial and any joys, sorrows or concerns that we might have. Those are the things that we can talk about with the person who is guiding our soul.

Ten Steps to Take

Americans are action-oriented. Whenever I lecture about the state of our society or point out certain problems, there is almost inevitably a student who asks, "What do I do? What procedures do I go through? What can we do?" I have listed at the bottom the kind of steps that I would say you need to take to really start to grow in virtue.

By the way, you do not have to do any of this. But as Socrates says at the end of the *Phaedo* if you have not used your time here to make resolutions or to start improving the way you live your life, then we have wasted our time here. If this book does not lead you to make some concrete resolutions to improve your life, then you have wasted your time reading it. I would almost say that these ten steps at the bottom are things you can try to go through almost on a daily basis or work on one thing at a time as a way of trying to grow or help yourself grow in virtue.

Realize that your life will truly start to make progress when you can learn to abandon yourself into God's hands, and have faith in him, and trust him. When you do that, you can start to learn to fearlessly examine your conscience. In other words, look at God, His Commandments, reality, and your circumstances in an objective way.

Whenever you realize you have done an injustice to anybody, whether it is to God or to another person, you should try to rectify that injustice.

Correcting vices

When you start to look at your conscience with respect to the virtues, it is likely that you will realize in many ways you are not living up to those virtues. Those shortcomings are defects. If you are habitually not living up to the virtues, those are called vices. You should have the disposition to want to lose those defects so as to acquire the virtues. If you want to lose those defects, one of the ways you start to lose them is to ask God to remove them.

We make amends to those we have harmed when we realize that we are wrong or that we have been ignorant about something. Or, if we are in error, we sincerely admit it, and we try to improve at that point. Someday you might be 40- or 70-years-old and realize "Gosh, there is this area of my life I have never tried to improve." What do you do at that point? Do you say, "Oh I am too old?" No! You say, "OK. Let's go."

That is not your dilemma now. Now your dilemma is to set out on the path of struggling to grow in virtue. This is what you can do right now to improve society in the long run. You might say, "I will work on that when I get out of college." That is a false attitude. With that attitude, you will at every moment of your life have an excuse to put off the struggle for another day. Whenever you realize you have a defect or vice you need to struggle with, that is the day that you should begin to struggle to uproot it and to acquire the opposite virtue.

To uproot that defect, you have to acquire the virtue that is opposing that vice. If you do not do that then you are not sincere. Because there is something that is in your heart or your thoughts, and your deeds are contradicting them.

Then finally, we start to learn how to pray every day, so that we can deepen our friendship with God. Deepening our friendship with God will enable us in the long term to deepen our friendship with others.

CHAPTER TWELVE

" **D**O ALL THINGS without grumbling or questioning, that you may be blameless and innocent, children of God without blemish in the midst of a crooked and perverse generation, among whom you shine as lights in the world, holding fast the word of life, so that in the day of Christ I may be proud that I did not run in vain or labor in vain." Phillipians 2:14-16

Conclusion

In this last chapter, there are a few things I want to go over. We have discussed the concept of leadership and how you can contribute to society as a leader. We have viewed relationships through the eyes of the ancient philosophers and the experiences of modern youth, and explored in depth the all-important relationship of friendship. We have gone over the structure of the modern university. We have gone over the typical pitfalls that befall freshman students. We have also gone over some basic attitudes and dispositions which can help you avoid these pitfalls. Finally, we have seen how the life of virtue, when you struggle to bring it about, can help one live happily in a difficult environment. One reason it is good to know all these things is that if you fall you can get up quicker.

The possibility exists that you have not implemented, or have tried but failed to implement virtue. In addition, you might fall in the future. You may not want to think about failure, but there is something to be said for knowing in advance how you are going to fall. When someone sins and starts doing illicit or immoral things, it can be very helpful if a good friend, without getting angry, goes to his friend and says, "You are doing such and such, you are free to do that. But remember, living without God is hard. A time might come when you will be filled with bitterness and resentment. You might be tempted to despair." In this situation, a friend might not be able to stop his friend from doing something harmful. But, he can, in a detached, patient, and affectionate way, explain to him the potential effects of his actions in advance. This kind of conversation can enable the potential evildoer to rethink his situation. It can also lay down the foundation for returning to the moral life.

There has to be some mentor you can find who will help you grow in virtue. Of course, there have been some young men who, after struggling to grow in virtue, decide that they do not want to do it anymore. And so they say, "Well, I am sick of you guys," and we say, "OK, great, so don't come for formation, don't pray, if you want to try that first semester, try it but you will find x, y and z. You'll find you'll get depressed, you won't be as happy, you'll have the sense that your life is getting out of control, you will lose that joy you had when you were praying." Then, as usually happens, people make a choice at some point: Do I come back, or do I continue down the rocky road to Dublin?

One goal in this book also has been to implant in your mind the idea of becoming a leader, and part of becoming a leader is obviously being a good student. Second, part of becoming a leader is that if you really want to transform society, you have to struggle to grow in virtue, seeing yourself as a servant of the common good, not a slave to consumer goods. Third, consider pursuing those kinds of careers where you can directly be of service to souls and the common good—politics, culture, media, journalism, education and so on. These are all ways in which you can greatly serve many souls in the course of your life.

Serving souls through your profession

The other day, after my classes, a student told me that he would love to be like Alfred Hitchcock and make horror films that would bring people back to morality. That would be a great way, a great career. Hitchcock admitted he was probably not going to be canonized, but he was a Catholic. If it is true, and I think it is, what Plato teaches, that art is the reflection of the soul of the artist, then all the more reason to set out on being the next Alfred Hitchcock. At the same time, while doing that, you should think about your soul, how to root out vice, how to grow in virtue, and how to make your soul a fertile field for God's grace.

Often when you get into cultural conversations people say, "We should not impose our faith into an art, whatever art is." In my opinion, in the end you do not have to worry about that. The fact is, every artist projects his soul into what he does. Every worker projects the order of his soul into the work he does. Every person projects his soul into his environment. There is a difference between taking personal responsibility for forming your soul, and requiring someone to have a deformed soul to enter into an industry. The man who wants you to not impose your faith on people could be essentially telling you that you have to deform your soul in order to enter into the marketplace. In this light, what you have to worry about is forming your soul.

When thinking about your role in the world, it might be helpful to read the *Letter to Diognetus*[2], part of which I quote here at length:

> Christians are indistinguishable from other men either by nationality, language or customs. They do not inhabit separate cities of their own, or speak a strange dialect, or follow some outlandish way of life. Their teaching is not based upon reveries inspired by the curiosity of men. Unlike some other people, they champion no purely human doctrine. With regard to dress, food and manner of life in general, they follow the customs of whatever city they happen to be living in, whether it is Greek or foreign.

> And yet there is something extraordinary about their lives. They live in their own countries as though they were only passing through. They play their full role as citizens, but labor under all the disabilities of aliens. Any country can be their homeland, but for them their homeland, wherever it may be, is a foreign country. Like others, they marry and have children, but they do not expose them. They share their meals, but not their wives.

> They live in the flesh, but they are not governed by the desires of the flesh. They pass their days upon earth, but they are citizens of heaven. Obedient to the laws, they yet live on a level that transcends the law. Christians love all men, but all men persecute them. Condemned because they are not understood, they are put to death, but raised to life again. They live in poverty, but enrich many; they are totally destitute, but possess an abundance of everything. They suffer dishonor, but that is their glory. They are defamed, but vindicated. A blessing is their answer to abuse, deference their response to insult. For the good they do they receive the

punishment of malefactors, but even then they rejoice, as though receiving the gift of life. They are attacked by the Jews as aliens, they are persecuted by the Greeks, yet no one can explain the reason for this hatred.

To speak in general terms, we may say that the Christian is to the world what the soul is to the body. As the soul is present in every part of the body, while remaining distinct from it, so Christians are found in all the cities of the world, but cannot be identified with the world. As the visible body contains the invisible soul, so Christians are seen living in the world, but their religious life remains unseen. The body hates the soul and wars against it, not because of any injury the soul has done it, but because of the restriction the soul places on its pleasures. Similarly, the world hates the Christians, not because they have done it any wrong, but because they are opposed to its enjoyments.

Christians love those who hate them just as the soul loves the body and all its members despite the body's hatred. It is by the soul, enclosed within the body, that the body is held together, and similarly, it is by the Christians, detained in the world as in a prison, that the world is held together. The soul, though immortal, has a mortal dwelling place; and Christians also live for a time amidst perishable things, while awaiting the freedom from change and decay that will be theirs in heaven. As the soul benefits from the deprivation of food and drink, so Christians flourish under persecution. Such is the Christian's lofty and divinely appointed function, from which he is not permitted to excuse himself.

The purpose of quoting the *Letter to Diognetus* is to illustrate that your work ultimately is a reflection of your soul, as you form your soul to grow into virtue, to be generous, to have a spirit of service, a spirit of sacrifice, to think of others and their comfort before you think of yourself and your comfort. St. Josemaria Escrivá used to say to young men your age, "To grow up and to be mature, pray and ask God that he grants you eighty years of gravity; not for you to be an old man and complain all the time but that you be that person because you are living a life of virtue."

The two great novelists of the 20th century, Flannery O'Connor and J.R.R Tolkien, had this ideal that they were not imposing their religion on their art. But they had well-formed souls. And so their art reflected their souls.

A lot of O'Connor's work is dark, but it is dark because she understands she is writing literature in an environment in which it might be good for her readers to think through the fragility of life, and to ask themselves whether the philosophies or ideologies that they have adopted will, in fact, enable them to be happy. She is not trying to write realistic stories. Her stories are almost allegories. She is trying to appeal to the Southern mind in a way that will lead people to the truth, and that will lead them to question some of the inconsistencies in their society as well as the modern mind.

One of her best stories is *The Lame Shall Enter First*. We see in it a conflict between the true and the good. O'Connor probably wrote it while reading Aquinas. She came to see that often in conflicts in the South, there is a tension between those who think what they are doing is good, but, in fact, this "good" is disassociated from the truth. Therefore, their goodness leads to bad fruits. On the other hand, in her books, there are those who think they have the truth, but they are incapable of doing what is good, also to disastrous consequences. Because she read Aquinas, because she was a sensitive observer of Southern culture, and because she was, quite frankly, a good writer, she could write stories that opened up to deeper questions about society and life. She projected the order of her soul into her art. This was not a form of force or coercion. In fact, many find her writings quite enjoyable, as are J.R.R. Tolkein's.

If you read her short stories as most literary critics do—as a reader following a realistic view and not trying to arrive at a deeper meaning, you will never understand O'Connor's message. The critics do not reach the deeper meaning as they lack the philosophy. Sometimes, they cannot see the deeper meaning because they themselves are rebelling against the moral order. They can only see in her writings what their souls allow them to see. This is not force or coercion. It is simply that they project their souls into what they do as well. Interestingly enough, the O'Connor readers who have little sense of morality, and cannot pick up on the truth that she is trying to write about, still respect her as a writer. They still identify her writings as impressive writing. O'Connor has the talent to write and her writing ultimately reflects her soul.

To some degree, the same artistic critique is true of Hitchcock. He is not overtly Catholic in his films, but in many of them he is presenting what happens when you break with the order of morality. He presents films which deal with these problems. Probably this is because in his soul he accepted the truth of the moral order. Again, he was not forcing himself on us. He was a great artist and the questions that moved his soul also moved his movies.

You are already in the world

The ultimate thing is not figuring out what your strategies are or how to work the Church into our environment or how to work the Church into society. As a matter of fact, you are in society, you are part of society, and you are already there. The question is how will you *be* there, or *what* will you be while you are there?

When St. Peter and St. John were first arrested by the Sanhedrin, they were told to no longer preach the name of Christ. Peter said to the Sanhedrin, "We will let you make your own judgment whether it is just or permitted for us, in the name of God, for us to speak the name of Christ in public. But we are going to keep on doing it because we think that God would be unjust to not let us speak about him in public."

That little passage in *Acts*, about the Sanhedrin's efforts to silence the Apostles, is the first moment in the separation of the Church and State. Basically, the Sanhedrin told the Apostles that they have to separate their faith from their public life and Peter says that is unjust.

You cannot force us to not speak about our faith. You cannot force us or trick us to not let our friendship with Christ influence our souls. Furthermore, you should not insinuate that somehow following Christ makes us less free than other men. You should not make us suspicious of the sources we want to go to in order to form our conscience. Why should I trust you, modern follower of Nietzsche, more than I trust my local spiritual director?

A quote from St. Augustine's *Confessions* is relevant:

> Being led, however, from this to prefer the Catholic doctrine, I felt that her proceeding was more unassuming and honest, in that she required to be believed things not demonstrated (whether it was that they could in themselves be demonstrated but not to certain persons, or could not at all be), whereas among the Manichees our credulity was mocked by a promise of certain knowledge, and then so many most fabulous and absurd things were imposed to be believed, because they could not be demonstrated.[3]

St. Augustine's text implies that the question you face in life is not whether to trust authority, it is what authority you should trust. There are those who will start out mocking authority, the possibility of knowledge, and casting aspersions on those who try to grow in virtue. It might seem interesting to follow such people in the beginning, because they claim to be enabling freedom.

But it is more honest, and more unassuming, to tell a person some things he has to accept, some things he can demonstrate. The purveyor of false freedom will, in the end, require you to accept all sorts of false, absurd and harmful things. The one who explains to you the nature of authority, reason, virtue, and the difficulty involved, is truly enabling your freedom. In the end, the mocker of virtue is the one who will force and coerce you. The one who tells you where you should trust and where you are on your own is enabling you to choose and act for yourself. This is the opposite of force. It is like the doctor who tells you what diseases you are disposed to so that you can avoid them.

We are already in society. Everybody else can speak about whatever they want. Why cannot we speak about our faith?

I came to this realization about Church and State when a freshman in college told me his story. Everyone talked about freedom, freedom, freedom, freedom, freedom. He began to think: "I want the freedom to form my conscience the way I want, and you cannot tell me what to do." He thought to himself, "What would happen if a politician would form his conscience as a Catholic just because he is using the best resources that are out there for him and acting according to his conscience? What if the Catholic position was the most rational? Would that mean that we should exclude from our conversations those who formed their conscience similar to what the Church teaches? Should we exclude the rational position, just because it happens to coincide with the teachings of Christ?" He suggested that in his philosophy classes and got silenced.

That is a fundamental point. If everyone else can say "I am going to Neitzsche (or Locke) to form my conscience," they are really not forming their conscience. They are acting on their passions and looking for authors who help them rationalize their disordered deeds. They are acting on their instincts, and then they say, "Well, that is my conscience, so you cannot stop me."

The problem is that these people tend to go one step further. At times, it seems as if they are seeking to eliminate from the university or from public discourse any source of conscience forming other than the ones they used. They cannot tolerate a Christian man using his freedom to form his conscience. In short, they are like the Sanhedrin when the Sanhedrin counseled Peter and John not to speak the name of Christ in public.

You are already in the world. You do not have to ask the question how to enter the world. You do have to ask the question how I am going to live in the world. The only people who really have to ask the question of how to enter the world are those who have joined religious orders and taken vows that, in effect, take them out of the world. But that is not your problem. You already are part of the world. You do not need to ask how to enter it. *You need to ask how you should live in the world.*

Perhaps if we learn to understand the problem correctly, answers more readily arise. You have just as much right to education and to have jobs in entertainment, media, journalism and politics as any other citizen of this country. Being Catholic or Christian does not make you an otherworldly person who, because of your baptism, has to be relegated to the status of a second class citizen. Perhaps due to historical struggles of the past centuries, Catholics too often have the mentality that they are not part of the world. This should be remedied.

If I could make a synopsis of Josemaria Escrivá on this point, it is that that the Christian spirit for laymen is that you are already in the world. Your problem is not how to figure out how to return to the world. You are already in the world. *Your problem is how to live in the world without being worldly.* Your problem is to live the virtues of the Christian gentleman without falling into the unjust, immoral practices of your time and of your society. In addition, it is your responsibility, using your ingenuity, training, money, and resources, to come up with the solutions to the problems that you see in the world. Only you can do this. And you can do this, if you set out to do it.

So living in the world is not a question of figuring out how to be normal or how to be like everybody else, because if you are just a baptized Christian, you already are like everybody else. You already are normal. The question is to figure out, "How do I really live as a Christian, how do I form my conscience so that I can truly say as this letter says that I am the soul of the world?"

The soul of the world

What the soul is to the body, Christians are to the world. The soul is distributed in every member of the body. Christians are scattered in every city in the world. The soul dwells in the body, and yet it is not of the body. Similarly, Christians live in the world, but they are not of the world.

The soul which is guarded in the visible body is not itself visible. So two Christians who are in the world are known, but their worship remains unseen. The flesh hates the soul and acts like an unjust aggressor because it is forbidden to indulge in pleasures. The world hates Christians not because they have done wrong but because they oppose its pleasures. The soul is locked up in the body and yet holds the body together. So Christians are held in the world as in a prison. And yet it is they who hold the world together.

We Christians are citizens like everybody else, we carry out our duties like everybody else; does; the difference is that we should have the freedom and, hopefully, also have the responsibility and maturity to truly live as Christian men. This oftentimes means going contrary to the ways of the world, especially in our own time where the typical ways of the world are exacerbated and the culture is forming everybody to become whatever they are desiring to become.

As you think about your time at the university, just think about your life. It is important to keep the *Letter to Diognetus* which is a model for Christian citizenship, because it is a model of how to live in the world. You live in the world by being primarily concerned about the formation of your soul so that you can in turn project your soul into your work and into your social environment and everything you do.

APPENDIX 1

Jansenism

JANSENISTS WERE CATHOLICS who tended to be overly rigoristic in their Catholicism. They were very much against the visible structures of the Church. And so, they often appealed to the sincerity of their individual conscience as the final appeal in matters of moral judgment. They tended to think that the visible structures of the Church were corrupt, that the true Church was the invisible Church, and that we should be suspicious of the visible structures of the Church. They were very rigorist in their morality, sometimes to an extreme. Some people claim that the Jansenists were like puritanical Catholics. That description confuses the situation. There were some principles of Jansenism that were condemned by the Church over the course of its several hundred years of existence.

Most of the Jansenists' principles had to do with excessive rigor in, for example, forgiving people's sins, in claiming that some sins were unforgivable and similar things.

Jansenists were somewhat like gnostics. Now, they had some positive points in their outlook. They were often scandalized by Catholics who would live a life of devotion, but who also lived corrupt lives at the same time—for example, someone who did not live the faith, but had the devotion of the Sacred Heart. Jansenists were scandalized sometimes by the kind of irrational reasoning of the Catholics, if, for example, some priest would figure out a way for a guy to go visit his mistress and then go to confession, and then go to communion and then go back to his mistress. The Jansenists were scandalized. That is what led them to excessive rigor.

So the Jansenists were not all that bad in wanting to uphold public morality and sound social order. They wanted to encourage Catholics not to be two-faced in the way they lived their faith. Liberation theology may be a good analogy. But there are some things about our economic arrangements that are completely unjust—the way we grind the poor, or the way we do not give people just wages; we think that economics is based on self interest. Most liberation theologians base their liberation theology foremost on critiquing these practices, which according to Catholic social doctrine are unjust. So that maybe would be a whole theology course. Jansenism versus Liberation Theology would be a *battle royale*. I do not think a lot of people would sign up for that course, but it would be an interesting one.

I once met a historian who has since died. After studying the French Revolution for about 40 years he concluded that if you really want to understand the French Revolution, you have to study Jansenism and how it became secularized; and that would give you the key to understanding the French Revolution. He died before he could finish his project. So if you like history you could make that your mission in life—understanding Jansenism and the French Revolution. You could revolutionize studies on the French Revolution.

Get Published, Inc!
Thorofare, NJ 08086
12 April, 2010
BA2010102